# Oracle BI Publisher 11g. A Practical Guide to Enterprise Reporting

Create and deliver improved snapshots in time of your Enterprise data using Oracle BI Publisher 11g

**Daniela Bozdoc**

BIRMINGHAM - MUMBAI

# Oracle BI Publisher 11g:
# A Practical Guide to Enterprise Reporting

First published: November 2011

Production Reference: 2011111

Published by Packt Publishing Ltd.
Livery Place
35 Livery Street
Birmingham B3 2PB, UK.

ISBN 978-1-84968-318-0

www.packtpub.com

Cover Image by Sandeep Babu (sandyjb@gmail.com)

# Credits

**Author**
Daniela Bozdoc

**Reviewers**
Chandan Banerjee
Brenner Grudka Lira
Michael Verzijl

**Acquisition Editor**
Stephanie Moss

**Development Editor**
Gaurav Mehta

**Technical Editors**
Llewellyn Rozario
Mehreen Shaikh

**Copy Editor**
Neha Shetty

**Project Coordinator**
Leena Purkait

**Proofreader**
Linda Morris

**Indexer**
Hemangini Bari

**Graphics**
Nilesh R. Mohite

**Production Coordinator**
Nilesh R. Mohite

**Cover Work**
Nilesh R. Mohite

# About the Author

**Daniela Bozdoc** is an IT professional with experience of almost a decade working as a software developer, an analyst, and a data and software architect on different technologies from MS .NET Framework to Sybase Power Builder, Oracle and MS SQL Server. She is continuing as an ERP consultant, and a report developer for MS dynamics NAV, Oracle EBS, and BI Publisher respectively in the present.

She is a graduate of Babes-Bolyai University of Cluj-Napoca, Romania, with a B.D. in Computer Science.

Daniela lives in Romania, where she has her family's support in her career and enjoys taking pictures of nature's beautiful landscapes.

I dedicate this book to my family for their unconditional love and support in every way possible throughout the process of writing this book and beyond. Their confidence in me especially has made this book a real thing.

I would like to express my gratitude to all those who gave me the opportunity to meet, and then to master, all the technology needed to write this book.

In addition, a special thanks to the people from Packt Publishing, editors, and project coordinators I worked with for their professionalism in offering me guidance and support.

# About the Reviewers

**Chandan Banerjee** is the Director and Principal Consultant at BA IT Consulting Pvt. Ltd. (www.baconsultinggroup.com).

He is also a partner and a Principal Consultant at Beetra Consulting (www.beetraconsultancy.com).

He has 20 years of experience in leading and deploying IT solutions out of which 18 years has been in the field of Business Intelligence (BI). He provides consulting services in BI Education, Data Integration, and Solution Architecture design. Managing deployments of common BI tools and applications are his forte. He is an expert in all phases of lifecycle development for business intelligence projects. He has also been the architect of two BI-based pre-built application products.

**Brenner Grudka Lira** has been a Business Intelligence Consultant at Apply Solutions since 2010. He has a bachelors degree in Computer Science from the Catholic University of Pernambuco in Recife, Brazil. He also has experience in building and modeling of data warehouses and has knowledge of Oracle Warehouse Builder, SQL Server Integration Services, SAP Business Objects, and Oracle Business Intelligence Standard Edition One. Today, he is dedicated to the study of business intelligence with a focus on ETL.

**Michael Verzijl** is a Business Intelligence consultant, specialized in OBIEE, BI Publisher, and Oracle Data Integrator.

Michael has a wide experience in the financial, utilities, and government industries that include BI technologies such as Oracle, IBM Cognos, and SAP Busines Objects.

He is currently employed as a Developer for the VX Company in Netherlands. Prior to this he was an employee of Accenture Technology Solutions and ING Investment Management.

I am thankful for the loving support of my wife Noortje and my son Joey.

# www.PacktPub.com

## Support files, eBooks, discount offers and more

You might want to visit www.PacktPub.com for support files and downloads related to your book.

Did you know that Packt offers eBook versions of every book published, with PDF and ePub files available? You can upgrade to the eBook version at www.PacktPub.com and as a print book customer, you are entitled to a discount on the eBook copy. Get in touch with us at service@packtpub.com for more details.

At www.PacktPub.com, you can also read a collection of free technical articles, sign up for a range of free newsletters and receive exclusive discounts and offers on Packt books and eBooks.

http://PacktLib.PacktPub.com

Do you need instant solutions to your IT questions? PacktLib is Packt's online digital book library. Here, you can access, read and search across Packt's entire library of books.

## Why Subscribe?

- Fully searchable across every book published by Packt
- Copy and paste, print and bookmark content
- On demand and accessible via web browser

## Free Access for Packt account holders

If you have an account with Packt at www.PacktPub.com, you can use this to access PacktLib today and view nine entirely free books. Simply use your login credentials for immediate access.

## Instant Updates on New Packt Books

Get notified! Find out when new books are published by following @PacktEnterprise on Twitter, or the *Packt Enterprise* Facebook page.

# Table of Contents

# Preface

In the last 15 years, some of us have witnessed mail becoming e-mail, grocery stores becoming www.store, and step-by-step technology becoming part of our daily life.

Technology development has radically changed the enterprise's way of doing business. First, daily tasks such as sales, client, and vendor management became computerized, and now all the resources are managed by enterprise applications. But this type of daily task support proved not to be enough for the business process, especially in the case of big organizations, which ended up with all kinds of applications, according to their vast field of activities. At some point they realized the need for some unified point of view. The choice was between replacing some applications and providing an integration process tool. Thus, **Business Intelligence (BI)** appeared in the scene. BI uses many types of data input, it doesn't take any note (if not necessary) of department, organization, or specific activities, and provides a unique answer for the corporate level.

Business Intelligence, in this way has become essential in most organizations. The goal in the near future is to support more effective business processes. Initially, it was used only for analysis and predictions based on the historical data; however, the new tendency of BI is to be actively involved in the business process. Integration seems to be the key to exploring the business possibilities, and providing the right tools seems to be the necessary step for an advanced business management.

In response to fast-growing demands, software development companies have come up with complex solutions, which can be used to plan, manage, and analyze a company's resources.

Somewhere in between, or being an active part for both the business process and software development, is the IT consultant. He has to stay in touch with the latest technologies, business solutions, and tools. He is an important factor when it comes to advising a company to adopt a new technology, a new tool, or a new vision concerning the IT field. There are two main categories of IT professionals involved in the process of providing these tools—the software developers and the report developers.

Having in mind the report developer's point of view, I will go through explaining the Business Intelligence concept—definition and process, Oracle BI, and finally an important component of Oracle BI—the Oracle BI Publisher—the document factory from Oracle.

# What is Business Intelligence?

**Business Intelligence** (**BI**) is the process of transforming data gathered from all the business data sources into decision support business information. Most companies gather data from their business activity, even using ERP and legacy applications with different databases. The amount of data input depends on the software tools used. Data characteristics depend on the company's structure, such as departments or activity profile. At this point, the complex process of data processing and formatting, which is necessary to generate even a simple report becomes visible. The need for a tool to process the amount of data gathered becomes visible, as well.

# Premises

The first thing that makes you think about a BI solution is the lack of information needed for the good course of the business process. Answers to questions such as these are very important:

- Which are my best suppliers?
- How much will it cost to start a new product's production?
- Where does all the money go?

The very first technical request to be accomplished is the data input quality. You won't have a good result if you have nothing to start with.

Another factor to be considered is the cost of a BI software implementation. This could be an expensive investment both from the perspective of time and financial resources.

# BI software application functions

For a software application to work as a BI solution, it has to provide tools for the following:

- Data mining
- OLAP (Online Analytical Processing)
- ETL (extract, transform, load)
- Predictive analytics
- Business performance management
- Reporting

The reporting tool has to be flexible enough to allow the creation of reports, charts, or dashboards along with running and scheduling them at different access levels. It has to allow reports viewing, printing, and saving in many formats. Integration with other products like Microsoft Office is also important.

# How it works

For a better understanding of how the described tools work together, take a look at the following figure:

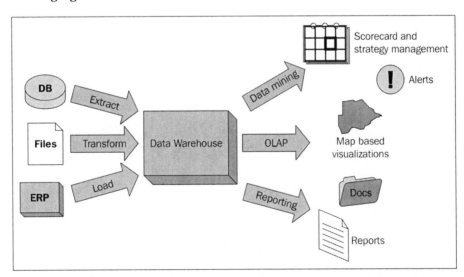

As you can see, the process begins with the corresponding data of the business. There are a lot of data sources types, such as databases and operational applications, and local data sources such as spreadsheets and XML files.

An ETL (or ELT, if you focus on Oracle Data Integrator) tool will perform the BI data integration process. In this way, the Data becomes accessible to the BI solution's end user.

The data warehouse is the central point of the BI solution. This contains structured data–detailed and consistent–for query analysis, and provides support for all BI operations from data mining to reporting. Unlike the Online Transaction Processing (OLTP) databases, data warehouses have a very different design to support a large amount of data (which does not need validation in this case), only a small number of users, and at the same time a particular access to the data depending on the particular queries that have to be processed. The historical data coming from business transaction processes is stored using a structure based on business entities, such as customer, product, and time.

The result of the business intelligence process is also visible through dashboards, analysis, reports, alerts, scorecards, and all these being available in a variety of designs and formats according to the end user requests.

# Business Intelligence software

As an introduction to the BI software world, here is a list of suggestions of actual software offers available in the market:

- Oracle BI
- SAP Business Objects
- Microsoft BI
- IBM
- SAS
- Microstrategy
- Actuate 7
- JasperSoft
- Olik View

# Oracle Business Intelligence

Among the leading industry of BI software, Oracle's solution was designed to address the entire spectrum of analytical requirements facing businesses including information access, analysis and reporting, and data integration and management.

Oracle's offer could be divided into two main categories of software:

- **Oracle BI Tools and Technologies**: It includes Oracle BI Foundation Suite, Oracle BI Enterprise Edition, Oracle Essbase, Oracle BI Publisher, Oracle Scorecard and Strategy Management, Oracle BI Standard Edition One, and Oracle Real-Time Decisions.

- **Oracle BI Applications**: These are built on OBIEE platform. Oracle BI Applications also include CRM Analytics and ERP Analytics applications. These solutions, being smart, agile, and aligned, will provide support for companies to achieve management excellence.

Oracle has also acquired Hyperion to expand their BI solution. The company claimed to be a leader in Enterprise Performance Management, by unifying Performance Management and BI solutions. It will support a broad range of strategic, financial, and operational management processes.

In the following sections, we will see how the Oracle BI solution maps to the Business Intelligence concept, including a short introduction to some Oracle BI components.

# Oracle Data sources

This refers to all data coming from sources interacting with the Oracle Business Intelligence server. Oracle BI supports Oracle Database, Oracle E-Business Suite and other Oracle based sources, IMB DB2 Database, Microsoft SQL Server, SAP NetWeaver BI, Microsoft Excel, flat files, ODBC sources, and XML data sources.

# Oracle Data Integrator

Data integration products are used to improve the speed of handling data, to reduce business process execution times, and to reduce development costs. Oracle Data Integrator combines all the elements of data integration to provide timely, accurate, and consistent information, which are as follows:

- Real-time and bulk data movement
- Transformation
- Synchronization
- Data quality
- Data management
- Data service

# Oracle BI Interactive Dashboards

**Oracle Dashboards** are in fact customized points of access for analytics information. According to the user's requests, the personalized information displayed is used in the decision making process. The resulting Web interface is provided to users according to their group membership and permissions.

# Oracle BI Server

This is the OLAP server. The **Oracle BI server** collects and aggregates information from all, even disparate data sources. It provides services to the other components, and processes the request, forming queries, and sending these queries to the underlying data source for processing. A very important factor in this case is the time of response, for the user to access immediately the answer to complex business questions, to be able to simulate various complex business scenarios

Oracle BI server is the heart that drives all the other components.

# Oracle BI Answers

Providing queries for the BI server, **BI Answers** is an ad hoc query and analysis tool. The web environment used is the gate to interactive charts, pivot tables, reports, and dashboards for the user. The user can save, modify, or format his view of information through the BI Answers tool.

# Oracle BI Delivers

Based on analytics results, **BI Delivers** creates alerts. Specified results can be detected within reports and the triggered alerts can be sent via multiple channels including e-mail, dashboards, and mobile devices. The notified dashboards can again trigger other alerts, resulting in a very close monitoring device for the business process.

Alerts are being sent to users based on a subscribing service.

# Oracle Scorecard and Strategy Management

This tool provides the ability to set a goal at the management level, to trace, and to apply all related activities involved in reaching the objective. The performance is monitored through **Key Performance Indicators (KPI)** , and many visualization types like KPI watch lists, maps, strategy trees, and diagrams are provided.

# Oracle BI Publisher

**Oracle BI Publisher** (formerly known as **XML Publisher**) is a reporting engine based on a very versatile open source language : XML. It can access relational, OLAP, and other data sources; in fact any data sources mapped to Oracle BI server.

It enables the creation, management, and delivery of all kinds of operational reports, financial reports, and any other customer-facing documents.

The result, consisting of high fidelity and highly formatted documents is delivered in a wide diversity of formats, such as: PDF, Excel, RTF, HTML, and electronic transfer documents. The results can be viewed online, saved for further processing, can be e-mailed, can be sent over FTP or scheduled for a delivery by, and for, a wide range of users and destinations.

However, the most important feature of Oracle BI Publisher is the fact that the report developer (not necessarily the software developer) is able to choose data sources and design the necessary reports.

The result types a user can get from Oracle BI are:

- Interactive dashboard: Provides with security, driven navigation
- Ad hoc analysis and interactive reporting: Provides with metrics, hierarchies, and calculations
- Enterprise reporting: It is provided by BI Publisher
- Proactive detection and alert: The alert engine can trigger workflows based on business events and notify stakeholders via their preferred medium or channel, such as: on the cell phone, via e-mail, a PDF file, or an Excel file
- Actionable Intelligence: The business process can be invoked from within the BI platform
- Microsoft Office integration: Information can be passed from Oracle BI to Microsoft Office documents such as Excel, Word, or Power Point
- Spatial Intelligence: It is provided via map-based visualization
- Scorecard and strategy management: Communicates strategic goals across the organization and monitors the process over time
- Server based query, reporting, and analysis: Provided by Oracle BI Server, which generates a query optimized from each data source, aggregates them, and presents the result.

# What this book covers

This book introduces Oracle Business Intelligence Publisher 11g, providing a suite of examples to help illustrate its main functionalities. Here is a synopsis of what you will find in the book:

*Chapter 1, What's New in Oracle BI Publisher 11g,* is a short presentation of Oracle BI Publisher 11g, with focus on the differences between the 10g release and the 11g release.

*Chapter 2, Creating a Data Model for a Report,* explains how Data Model Editor – the new feature provided by BI Publisher 11 – looks and works.

*Chapter 3, Multiple Data Sources,* describes how BI Publisher retrieves and structures the data used for a report.

*Chapter 4, Report Layout Template,* is about data presentation, which include layout types, visual components of the report, and template types.

*Chapter 5, The New XPT Format* introduces the new report format used by Oracle BI Publisher 11g. It generates almost pixel perfect output and could be a good substitute for PDF forms.

*Chapter 6, Oracle BIP Template Builder for Microsoft Word,* describes layout designing in MS Word.

*Chapter 7, The Report Cconfiguration,* demonstrates how reports are managed, and how to view, run, or set properties for reports.

*Chapter 8, Exploring BI Publisher 11g: A Simple Report Example,* is a simple report example. It presents an example, covering all the steps described in the previous chapters.

*Chapter 9, BI Publisher 11g and E-Business Suite,* discusses integration with Oracle e-Business Suite.

*Appendix A, Report Translations,* is a walk through all the translation techniques that BI Publisher offers.

*Appendix B, Migrating Oracle Reports to BI Publisher,* describes the steps required to migrate Oracle Reports to BI Publisher Reports.

*Appendix C, Debugging Oracle Reports to BIP Migration,* deals with an error that frequently occurs in Oracle Reports to BIP migration process. The neccesary steps required to correct this type of error are described here.

*Appendix D, Glossary,* a short list of BI Publisher specific terms, for a better understanding of the concepts explained.

# What you need for this book

You need to have the following:

- A database installed. Supported database types include Oracle Database, Microsoft SQL Server, and IBM DB2
- Oracle Business Intelligence schemas installed using Repository Creation Utility (RCU) 11.1.1.3.
- You need to have access to Oracle BI Publisher 11g (installed as stand alone or as part of Oracle Business Intelligence Enterprise Edition 11g)
- BIPublisher_11.1.1.3_Desktop
- Microsoft Word
- Microsoft Excel
- Adobe Reader
- An HTML Browser (Internet Explorer 7.0 or above, or Mozilla Firefox 3.6.3 or above recommended)

# Who this book is for

Reports are often the most visible output of a software application, with a great impact for the decisional process. So it is very important that the information on a report is accurate. Providing this is the **report developer** who has to be skilled in both designing the layout for the report and understanding the report's data sources.

Although, there is no need to have prior experience with BI Publisher 11g to read this book, it is desirable for a report developer to know the basics of SQL, entity-relationship model (ERM), programming logic, and concepts of BI.

# Conventions

In this book, you will find a number of styles of text that distinguish between different kinds of information. Here are some examples of these styles, and an explanation of their meaning.

Code words in text are shown as follows: "You can see the distinctive parts of the data template file, such as: `dataQuery` containing SQL statements and `dataStructure` containing groups and elements."

A block of code is set as follows:

```
<?xml version="1.0" encoding="UTF-8" ?>
<dataTemplate name="AR_RECEIPT" version="1.0">
<properties>
```

**New terms** and **important words** are shown in bold. Words that you see on the screen, in menus, or dialog boxes for example, appear in the text like this "clicking the **Next** button moves you to the next screen".

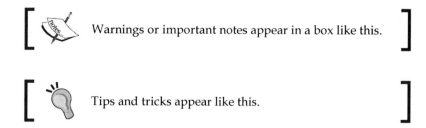

Warnings or important notes appear in a box like this.

Tips and tricks appear like this.

# Reader feedback

Feedback from our readers is always welcome. Let us know what you think about this book–what you liked or may have disliked. Reader feedback is important for us to develop titles that you really get the most out of.

To send us general feedback, simply send an e-mail to feedback@packtpub.com, and mention the book title via the subject of your message.

If there is a book that you need and would like to see us publish, please send us a note in the **SUGGEST A TITLE** form on www.packtpub.com or e-mail suggest@packtpub.com.

If there is a topic that you have expertise in and you are interested in either writing or contributing to a book, see our author guide on www.packtpub.com/authors.

# Customer support

Now that you are the proud owner of a Packt book, we have a number of things to help you to get the most from your purchase.

# Errata

Although we have taken every care to ensure the accuracy of our content, mistakes do happen. If you find a mistake in one of our books—maybe a mistake in the text or the code—we would be grateful if you would report this to us. By doing so, you can save other readers from frustration and help us improve subsequent versions of this book. If you find any errata, please report them by visiting http://www.packtpub.com/support, selecting your book, clicking on the **errata submission form** link, and entering the details of your errata. Once your errata are verified, your submission will be accepted and the errata will be uploaded on our website, or added to any list of existing errata, under the Errata section of that title. Any existing errata can be viewed by selecting your title from http://www.packtpub.com/support.

# Piracy

Piracy of copyright material on the Internet is an ongoing problem across all media. At Packt, we take the protection of our copyright and licenses very seriously. If you come across any illegal copies of our works, in any form, on the Internet, please provide us with the location address or website name immediately so that we can pursue a remedy.

Please contact us at copyright@packtpub.com with a link to the suspected pirated material.

We appreciate your help in protecting our authors, and our ability to bring you valuable content.

# Questions

You can contact us at questions@packtpub.com if you are having a problem with any aspect of the book, and we will do our best to address it.

# 1
# What's New in Oracle BI Publisher 11g?

Oracle BI Publisher (formerly known as Oracle XML Publisher) is Oracle's reporting XML-based technology, which generates highly formatted data output using multiple data sources. It was originally developed to solve the reporting problems faced by Oracle Applications, released as a standalone version, and finally it also became a part of the Oracle BI Enterprise Edition as Oracle BI Publisher. Starting with the 11g version, Oracle BI Publisher was completely redesigned to incorporate new functionalities. In this chapter, we will be covering the following topics:

- A comparison with 10g
- Getting started with Oracle BI Publisher 11g
- Backward compatibility of BI Publisher 11g with BI Publisher 10g reports

## A comparison with 10g

The new 11g release of Oracle BI Publisher introduces some new features highly anticipated and desired by both reports' developers and the reports' end users. Let's take a look at the major improvements brought about with the new release.

## Building a Data Model

In the 10g release, for a **data definition** you had to create an XML configuration file containing both data sources definition and XML structure definition. For example, this code is written using notepad:

**Downloading the example code**

You can download the example code fi les for all Packt books you have purchased from your account at http://www.PacktPub.com. If you purchased this book elsewhere, you can visit http://www.PacktPub.com/support and register to have the fi les e-mailed directly to you.

```
<?xml version="1.0" encoding="UTF-8" ?>
<dataTemplate name="AR_RECEIPT" version="1.0">
<properties>
  <property name="xml_tag_case" value="upper" />
  <property name="debug_mode" value="on" />
</properties>
<parameters>
  <parameter name="P_CASH_RECEIPT_ID" dataType = "number"></parameter>
</parameters>
<dataQuery>
  <sqlStatement name="Q_RECEIPT">
SELECT acr.cash_receipt_id, acr.amount, acr.currency_code, acr.
receipt_number, to_char(acr.receipt_date, fnd_profile.value('ICX_DATE_
FORMAT_MASK'))
receipt_date, acr.pay_from_customer, acr.deposit_date, hp.party_name,
hp.address1 || ' ' || hp.address2 client_address, ar_receipt_string.
rows_to_string, xxrop_string.currency_to_string(acr.amount) words
FROM ar_cash_receipts_all acr, hz_cust_accounts hca, hz_parties hp
WHERE acr.cash_receipt_id=:P_CASH_RECEIPT_ID AND acr.pay_from_customer
= hca.cust_account_id AND hca.party_id = hp.party_id
  </sqlStatement>
   <sqlStatement name="Q_SIGNATURE">
    <![CDATA[  SELECT   user_name FROM fnd_user, fnd_concurrent_
requests
         WHERE REQUESTED_BY = user_id and CONCURRENT_PROGRAM_ID =
fnd_global.conc_program_id() and request_id = fnd_global.conc_request_
id() ]]>
  </sqlStatement>
  <sqlStatement name="Q_MO">
    <![CDATA[ SELECT   fnd_profile.value('COMPANY_NAME') org_name FROM
dual ]]>
  </sqlStatement>
</dataQuery>
<dataStructure>
    <group name="G_SIGNATURE" dataType="varchar2" source="Q_
SIGNATURE">
      <element name="REP_AUTHOR" dataType="varchar2" value="user_
name"/>
    </group>
    <group name="G_MO" dataType="varchar2" source="Q_MO">
      <element name="COMPANY_NAME" value="org_name"/>
    </group>
```

```
      <group name="G_REC" source="Q_RECEIPT">
        <element name="NUMBER" value="receipt_number" />
        <element name="REC_DATE" value=" receipt_date " />
        <element name="AMOUNT" value="amount" />
        <element name="CURRENCY" value="currency_code" />
        <element name="CLIENT" value="party_name" />
        <element name="CLIENT_ADDRESS" value="client_address" />
      </group>
  </dataStructure>
  </dataTemplate>
```

You can see the distinctive parts of the data template file, such as, `dataQuery` containing SQL statements and `dataStructure` containing groups and elements.

With the new release of BI Publisher, you don't need to see and edit XML templates anymore. The new web-based user interface makes it all visual. The Data Model Editor provides tools to build queries, define the data structure, and create formulae from different data sources, as you can see in the following screenshot:

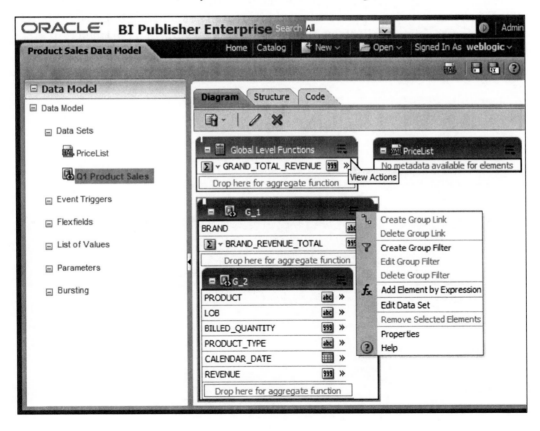

Another advantage of the Data Model is that it now has a life of its own. A Data Model can be saved and, afterwards, used as many times as you like, increasing reusability and data quality. Compared to 10g, where a Data Model couldn't be reused, this is a great new feature.

# Designing a layout

In BI Publisher 10g, the **layout template** can be designed using external tools such as: Microsoft Word, Adobe Acrobat, Microsoft Excel, and Adobe Flash. Templates created using these tools contain embedded fields with properties that determine how the XML data will be merged into the template. Using a combination of native Microsoft Word features and BI Publisher command syntax, you can create a report template that is ready to accept XML data from your system. You have to choose the desired tool to build the data template according to the design specifications and final output type.

For example, RTF templates can generate the following output types: PDF, HTML, RTF, Excel, Power Point, zipped PDF, and MHTML. The following screenshot shows how you can assign an XML element (this could be a formula or a parameter) to a report field in the template builder for Word:

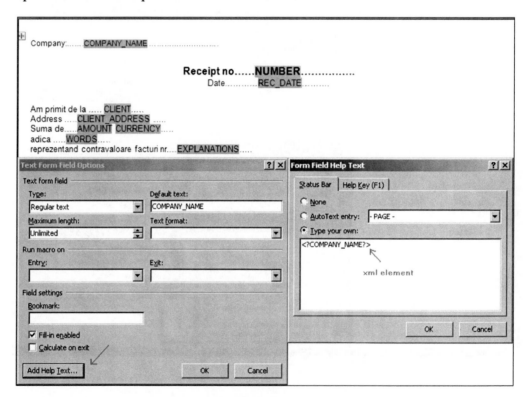

Double click on the **Text form field** to get the **Text Form Field Options** window and then click the **Add Help Text** button to get the **Form Field Help Text** window.

You can load a sample XML and you have tools to support adding tables, pivot tables, charts, grouping and formatting data, and also to preview the final result.

But with the arrival of BI Publisher 11g, the layout template definition changed radically—a web-based **layout editor** was introduced. This can generate pixel perfect reports, and the most exciting part is that you can interact with data allowing re-sorting and filtering of existing reports. Clicking on any section of a component such as Table, Chart, Pivot Table, or Gauge refreshes other linked components in the report to reflect the selection, without refreshing the whole report or page.

In the following screenshot, you can see the correspondence created between the right side chart where I have the total revenue divided by quarters, and the left side chart where revenues for only one quarter is displayed. The link created between these two entities allows you to interactively change the values from the **Quarterly Sales Revenue** by clicking the desired quarter on the **Percent(%) Revenue by Quarter** chart:

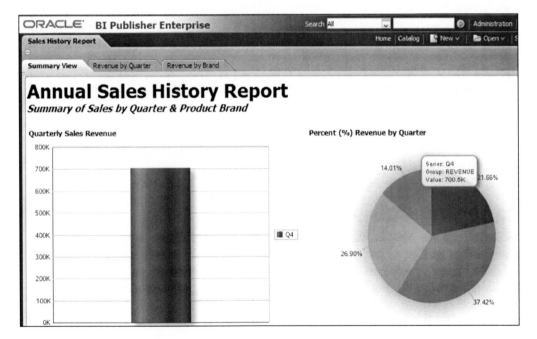

You can add multiple templates of different types to your report, whereas with 10g you had to use many reports containing the same data. Now with 11g you can include many data perspectives in one report, and have many output types attached to the same report.

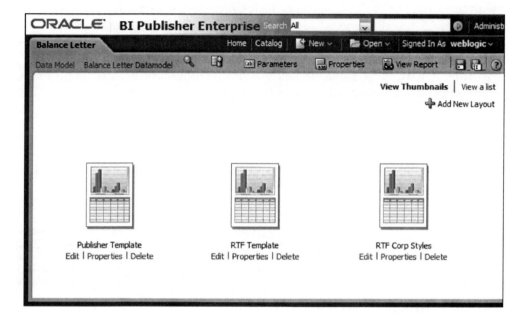

The different types of templates are shown in the preceding screenshot.

There are a few more features introduced/ improved upon by the BI Publisher 11g release. These include:

# Managing sub-templates

For defining a reusable formatting functionality in BI Publisher, a **Subtemplate** can be defined in an RTF or an XSL file format. Previously the sub-templates were saved and called from an external directory; but with the new release, sub-templates are considered catalog objects and are saved and managed in the catalog.

# Style templates

Also managed in the BI Publisher catalog are the newly introduced **Style Templates**. To keep the company identity intact across all company reports, a style template can be applied to RTF layouts. You can see an example style template in the following screenshot:

## Custom Title

### Heading 1

*Heading 2*

## Custom Heading1

*Custom Heading2*

Style Name: Table Style1

| Column 1 | Column 2 | Column 3 |
|----------|----------|----------|
| West | 234 | 567 |
| East | 786 | 987 |

Style Name: Table Style2

| Column 1 | Column 2 | Column 3 |
|----------|----------|----------|
| West | 234 | 567 |
| East | 786 | 987 |

# Zipped PDF

The BI Publisher 11g release also introduces a new output type: **PDFZ** or zipped PDF. The purpose was to have smaller and more manageable files instead of a large PDF output file. So when PDF output splitting is enabled for a report, this file is split into multiple files generated in one zip file. An index file is also created with *from/to* in it.

# Scheduling a report job

Another thing improved from the previous release is the **scheduling options**. Now you can schedule multiple outputs for a report with a different layout applied as you can see in the following screenshot and send each output to a different destination. Also to define schedule times, there are now more recurrence pattern options:

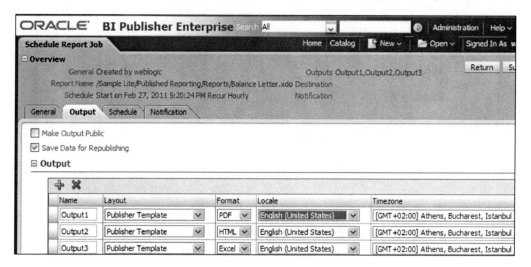

# Getting started with Oracle BI Publisher 11g

The main components for working with Oracle BI Publisher are:

- **Data query**: This engine formats XML data provided by any system that can generate XML, including web services and any data available through **Java DataBase Connectivity (JDBC)**.

- **Layout template**: This defines the layout format. The layout template can be designed using Microsoft Word, Adobe Acrobat, Microsoft Excel (standalone version), Adobe Flash (standalone version), and Oracle BI Publisher's own layout editor.

- **Report definition**: This brings together the query and one or more templates, which you will see in the *Layout Options* section of this chapter.

- **Report jobs**: This means submitting, scheduling, and delivering reports to multiple destinations.

To start with, let's take a tour through BI Publisher's interface components.

# BI Publisher homepage

Starting on the homepage, it is very easy to see all of the main actions that you can proceed with. You can create a new:

- **Report**
- **Report Job**
- **Data Model**
- **Style Template**
- **Sub Template**

You can also browse the existing ones.

 You can access the current running jobs from the **Report Jobs** link, and completed jobs from **Report Job History**.

In this screenshot, the central section shows a list of **Recent** accessed objects:

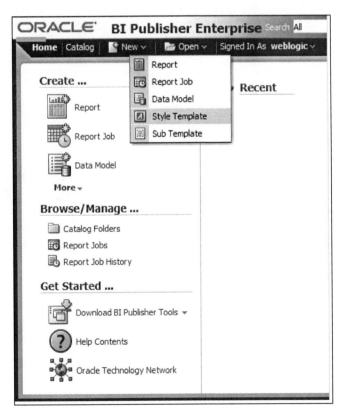

# Catalog

For browsing existing entities, you must open the **Catalog**. The **Catalog** page contains a tree-like structure of folders of all the elements created in BI Publisher. It is, in my opinion, a very friendly interface which enables quick access to general actions (available for any kind of component), such as **Delete**, **Copy**, **Cut**, **Rename**, and so on, and also to specific actions. For example, when you look at a report you can see that a report can be opened, scheduled, and edited, or its submissions tracked in **Jobs** or **Jobs History** lists.

Notice the **Search** bar on the top, where you can search through **All** entities, or you can select other categories of entities to search through:

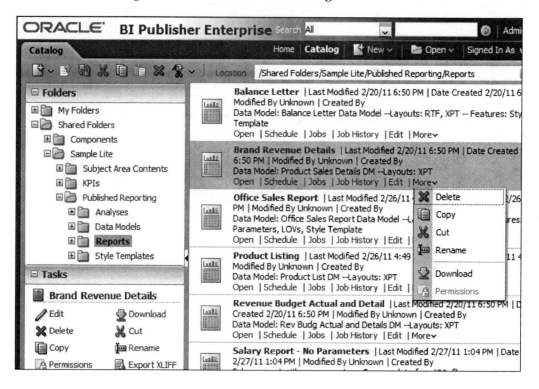

Let's browse the catalog to find and edit an existing Data Model.

# Data Model Editor

The **Data Model Editor** provides tools to choose various types of data sources and to build the desired model and structure of data. For data type sources, you can choose one or more from: SQL query, MDX query, Oracle BI Analysis, view object, web service, LDAP query, XML file, Microsoft Excel file, and HTML (XML Feed).

As you can see in the left section of the next screenshot, you can attach the following to a Data Model:

- **Data Sets**: Contains the Data Model query structure
- **Event Triggers**: Triggers to be executed before or after the report
- **FlexFields**: Oracle EBS Flexfields
- **List of Values**: LOV's for parameters
- **Parameters**: Report variables, which are requested by the report at runtime
- **Bursting options**: Setup of bursting destinations

These options will be addressed in much more detail in *Chapter 2, Creating a Data Model for a Report.*

To design your Data Model query structure, the Data Set editor presents three different approaches:

- **Diagram view**: This enables data grouping, entities linking, sorting, and calculations
- **Structure view**: This allows you to assign a name to each XML element that will be displayed in the final layout, and to assign values in case of NULL values or to change data types
- **Code view**: This provides the XML structure

For example, to create a SQL Data Set, you must choose the Data Source (from all the options available in the data source list) and provide the SQL query. But we'll go into more detail with this in *Chapter 3, Multiple Data Sources,* of this book.

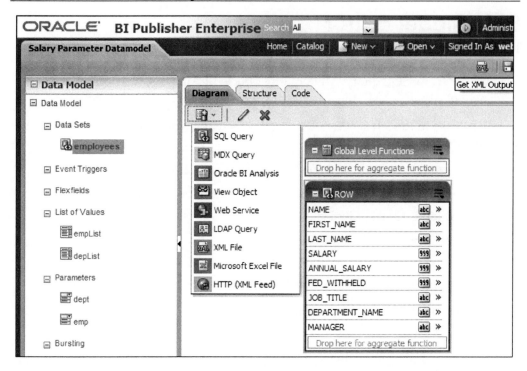

After creating the Data Model, there is another feature you can take advantage of, that is, you can generate a sample XML data by accessing the **Get XML output** option, which is shown in the preceding screenshot. In this way, you will be able to take a first look at the generated data, and afterwards test your layout template.

# Layout options

Once you have built the desired Data Model, you can start building the report. First, you have to choose the template designer type to use. This is somehow a difficult task to complete because you have to take the following into consideration:

- The tools offered by each template designer (depending on the template type you choose from those specified in the next screenshot)
- The desired output, requested in specifications

As shown in the next screenshot, choosing a template type from the **Create Layout** section will trigger BI Publisher's own layout editor. Newly available in the BI Publisher 11g release, templates can be created, edited, and viewed online. But, you still have the option to build your template using an external tool. From the **Upload or Generate Layout** section, you can access an interface for browsing and uploading these types of template files:

- RTF
- PDF
- Excel
- Flash
- XSL Stylesheets
- eText

An RTF template can also be simply generated. In this case, **BI Publisher (BIP)** will actually create a default layout for you, which includes all the fields specified in your Data Model:

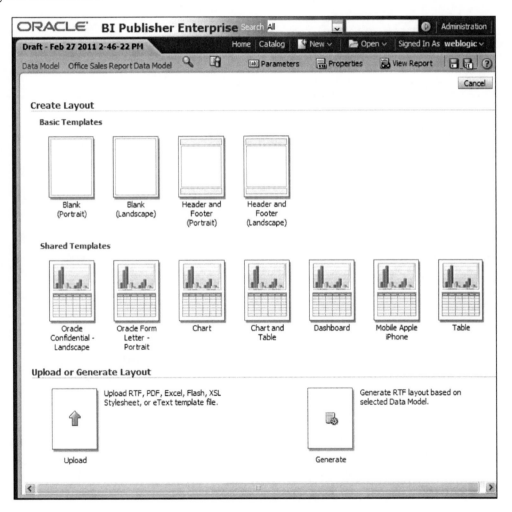

# Template builder for Word

To edit a BIP template using Template Builder for Word, you have the option of logging into BIP to choose and open the desired template.

Once all modifications are complete, the template can be uploaded back into BIP by following the menu function **Upload Template**. The Template Builder will import your changes back into the BIP report definition.

Using the Template Builder for Word you can build an RTF template as shown in the following screenshot:

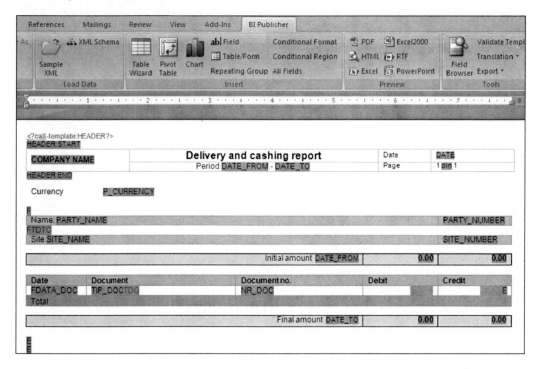

To map the template field to the XML element data field, a **placeholder** is created. At runtime the placeholder is replaced by the value of the element with the same name in the XML data file. A more in-depth description of the methodology will follow later in the book, in *Chapter 6, Oracle BIP Template Builder for Microsoft Word*.

Finally, on opening the created report, BI Publisher immediately displays the results obtained by applying the attached templates against the chosen Data Model. As you can see in the next screenshot, for the current report You have five layouts defined in tabs:

- **Simple**
- **Advance Page Totals**
- **Batch Manager Salary**
- **W-2 2010 (Partial)**
- **Manager Summary**

Each tab page contains a report layout, depending on the number of attached templates:

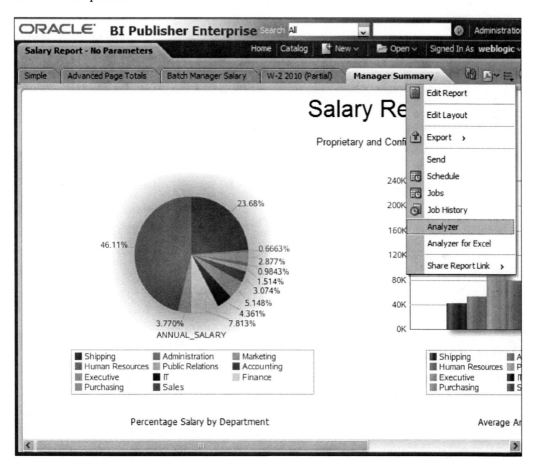

From here, you can further edit the report or the layout, or export, send, or schedule the report, but you also have access to an another interesting BI Publisher feature: the Online Analyzer.

# The Online Analyzer

The **Online Analyzer** enables you to create ad hoc pivot views of your data. In a pivot table structure, you can drag and drop data elements, which can be afterwards arranged, filtered, and summarized. You can see in the next screenshot the interface offered to build a pivot table.

You can save your pivot table as a layout for your report by exporting it and saving it as a BI Publisher layout. The export command saves the pivot table as the BI Publisher layout type (.xpt). It will then have all the features and properties of a BI Publisher layout:

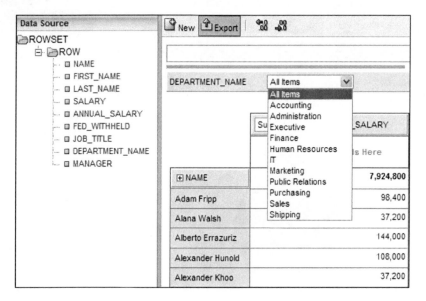

# Schedule report job

Besides having the report running online, you can also schedule the report. Using the **Schedule Report Job** page, you can submit a report job with precise parameters, define multiple outputs for a scheduled job, and add different delivery destinations. The BI Publisher interface provides four tabs to input Report Job parameters, as shown in the next screenshot:

- On the **General** tab you have to choose the report name and input its parameters.

- On the **Output** tab you can choose to:

  ◦ Use a bursting definition to determine the output and delivery destination. This option is available only if the report has a bursting definition and disables all the other fields on the page.

- Make the output public. The output will be available to all users with access to the report.

- Save the data for republishing, that is, save the XML data.

On the same tab, in the output table, you can add multiple outputs, that is, you have to set output parameters: **Name**, **Layout**, **Format**, **Locale**, **Timezone**, and **Calendar**. Multiple destinations can also be set for the report to be delivered to. There are five destination types:

- Email

- Printer

- Fax

- FTP

- HTTP

- On the **Schedule** tab, schedule times are defined. You can set a combination of parameters between: **Frequency**, **Every**, **On**, **Start**, **End**, **Right now**, and **On a fixed day**.

- The **Notification** tab allows you to configure a notification to be sent by e-mail or HTTP when the report is **Completed**, is **Completed with warnings**, or **Failed**:

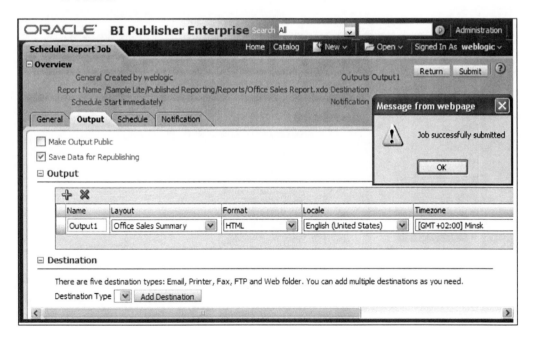

# Bursting options

Bursting definitions are defined in the Data Model design interface.

**Bursting** is a process of splitting data into blocks. For each block of the data, a separate document is generated and delivered to one or more destinations. For the delivery, based on an element in the Data Model, you can have different templates, output format, delivery method, or locale.

On the **Bursting** page you have to set a few parameters, as shown in the next screenshot:

- **Split by**: An element from the Data Set, used to split the data
- **Deliver By**: An element from the Data Set, used to format and deliver the data
- **SQL Query**: Provides the required information to format and deliver the report parameters

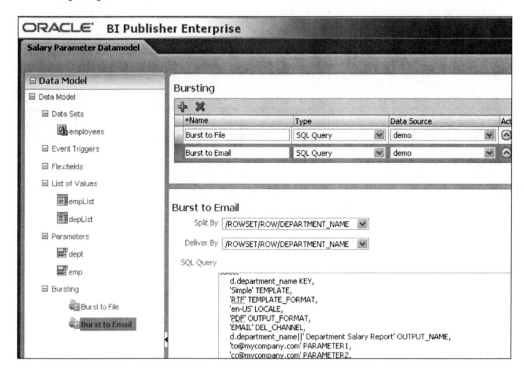

# Report job history

The following is the **Report Job History** page, which displays information about running report jobs and completed report jobs. In the first place, this page provides a filter list to facilitate report job searching.

A matching criteria jobs list will be displayed and from the **Report Job Histories** list you will be able to do the following:

- View the status and details of running and completed report jobs. For this click on the **Report Job Name** drop-down.
- Download or view the report XML data.
- Download or view the report document.
- Republish the report data.
- Delete report jobs from history.

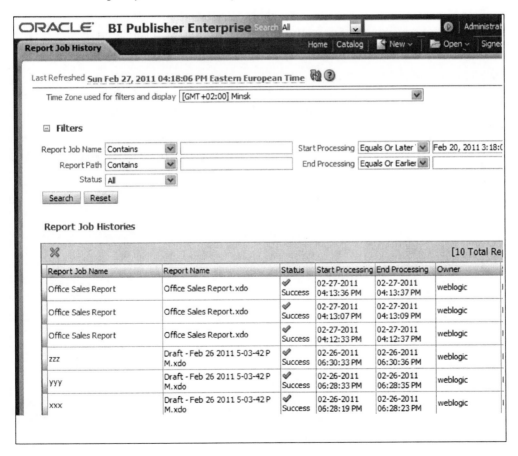

# Integrated thin-client report design editor

You have a complete set of tools to provide multiple layouts for your data, grouped into three tabs, as shown in the following screenshot:

In the **Insert** tab, you can choose to insert components such as:

- **Chart**
- **Data Table**
- **Pivot table**
- **Layout grid**
- **Gauge**

In the **Page Layout** tab, you can set the page orientation and insert the page footer or header.

The third tab is contextual and contains characteristics that one can set for the current selected component. For example, for a text field you can set font characteristics and alignment.

Data elements available on the left side of the layout editor are added into the desired structure by simply dragging-and-dropping it into the designated locations. Notice these very useful hints: **Drop Value Here** or **Drop Label Here**:

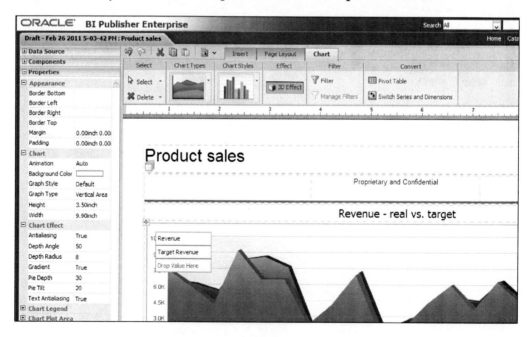

A complete list of properties can be accessed on the left side too, as shown in the next screenshot. **Gauge** properties list is shown in this example:

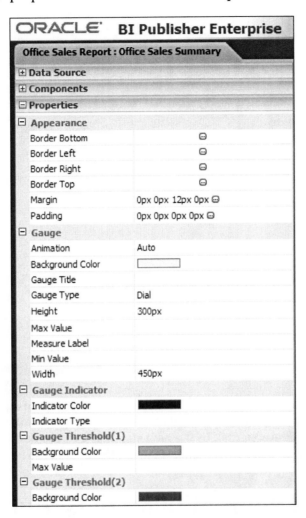

To complete the new features list, let's see how the **Interactive Viewer**, which is the most exciting new feature added in the 11g release works, by making different components on the report page interact. This is only a short introduction of this feature, and we'll discuss this in detail in *Chapter 5, The New XPT Format.*

In the following screenshot, on the **Page Layout** tab you have the **Configure Events** option, which triggers the **Configure Events** interface:

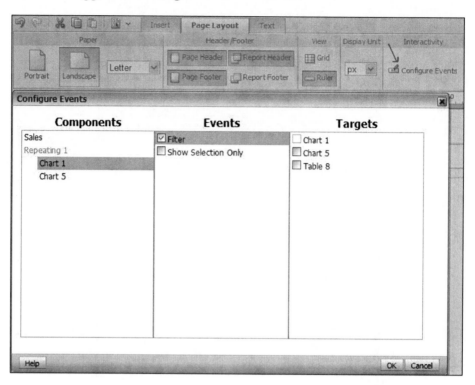

As you can see in this screenshot, the **Configure Events** interface adds layout components to the **Components** list (only if they can trigger events) and to the **Targets list** (all the components). In the next step, the user creates links between elements belonging to these two categories using the **Events** list.

# Backward compatibility of BI Publisher 11g with BI Publisher 10g reports

Seeing all these new great features, you may be asking how much trouble it would be to upgrade your work to the BIP 11g release?

But once BIP 11g is installed, Oracle provides the **upgrade assistant utility** to upgrade the repository and web catalogs.

When moving from 10g to 11g, we will have to use the upgrade utility because the repository structure and the web catalog structure have changed a lot between the different versions.

>  A direct copy and paste into the 11g version will not work, so the upgrade assistant utility must be used.

# Summary

Oracle Business Intelligence Publisher 11g proves to be a great reporting solution, generating any kind of data output you might need. The following are among the strengths of the new release:

- Various data sources types
- Incorporated Data Model designer
- Separation of the Data Model from the report layout
- Incorporated layout editor
- A great variety of output formats
- Interactive viewer
- Multiple possible destinations
- Report jobs scheduler
- Report translations support

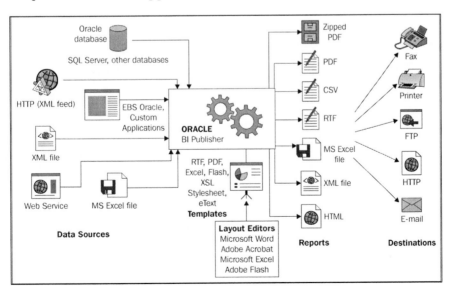

As the preceding figure reveals, BI Publisher can query or accept data from different data sources like databases, web services, HTTP feeds, or file data. BI Publisher structures the input data in an XML-based format, applies a format against it, and delivers it to the end users.

BI Publisher layout templates can be designed using Microsoft Word, Microsoft Excel, Adobe Acrobat, Adobe Flash tools or its own layout designer.

It is a tool that can efficiently generate thousands of pre-formatted documents like invoices, financial statements, sales reports, and so on, per hour with minimal impact to transactional systems. Reports can be published to different output formats and delivered in environments like online reports, e-mail, printers, faxes, FTP, and HTTP.

In the next chapter, you'll learn to work with the Data Model Editor to configure and use multiple data source types for your reports.

# 2
# Creating a Data Model for a Report

The **Data Model** is a new concept introduced in BIP 11g. Using the Data Model Editor, you can choose multiple data sources for your reports. You can also create and refine elaborate structures of data to extract XML report data from, and attach report-connected entities as event triggers or parameters.

In this chapter, we will see the components of a Data Model. We will see in detail how each component is addressed by the BIP Data Model Editor with the help of a few examples, which will give us a better understanding of the way the Data Model builder works.

## Report Data Model Editor interface

To get to the Data Model Editor interface go on the BIP **Home** page and select **Data Model** from the **Create** section. Alternatively, you can click **New** on the **Catalog** page and select **Data Model** from the drop-down menu.

You'll get the **Properties** page displayed as shown in the following screenshot. On this page, you can set multiple report characteristics, such as:

- **Description**: This is your Data Model description.
- **Default Data Source**: To get access to multiple data sources to design your report data structure. All the data sources that you want to use must be configured. You must go to **Administration**, the link on the upper-right corner of the screenshot. Data sources configuration and multiple data sources will be widely discussed in the next chapter.
- **Oracle DB Default Package**: This will be the default package to look for the event triggers.

- **Backup Data Source**: This name can be used if the default data source is not available.
- **XML output options**: There are three options provided. You can select the most suitable options to fit your work needs. For example, you check only the **Include Parameter Tags** option depending upon your needs.
- **XML Tag Display**: The possible options are: **Upper Case**, **Lower Case**, and **Follow the Data Structure**:

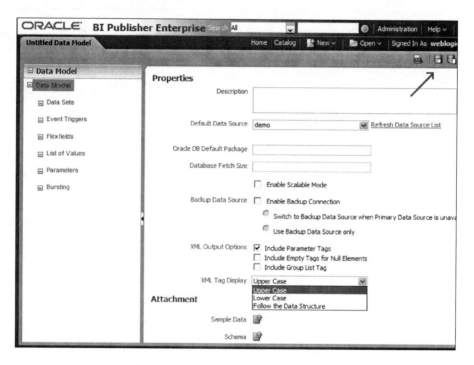

On the upper-right corner you may notice a few icons. These are the shortcuts to manage your Data Model. For example, you can preview the XML data for the Data Model and save the current Data Model.

Through the interface provided for the XML data preview, the XML data can be viewed, exported, or saved as sample data. In this case, it will be listed in the **Sample Data** section of the interface as shown in the previous screenshot. This is helpful when designing and testing the layout templates.

The main functionality of the Data Model Editor interface is to provide tools that help you to build your data structure, aggregate data, customize data, and do different calculations. This is available in the **Data Sets** section of the Data Model. But there are also a few elements required by the report (both at design and at run time), such as:

- Event Triggers
- Flexfields
- List of Values (LOVs)
- Parameters
- Bursting options

Let's go deeper into these components and their functionality.

# Data Sets

As you can see in the following screenshot, the available data set types are:

- **SQL Query**
- **MDX Query**
- **Oracle BI Analysis**
- **View Object**
- **Web Service**
- **LDAP Query**
- **XML file**
- **Microsoft Excel File**
- **HTTP (XML Feed)**

To add a particular Data Set to your data structure, containing one of the types described in the previous screenshot, you first have to provide some parameters, which depending on the Data Set type, precisely identify your data.

# Data Set types

Let's go through the steps required to add data sets of the most common types:

## SQL query

To configure a SQL Query Data Set you have to enter the following, which is shown in the following screenshot:

- **Name**: Data set name of your choice
- **Data Source**: Choose a data source from the list (data sources added using the Administration interface)
- **SQL Query**: Within BIP's Data Model Editor, queries may be manually coded or created using **Query Builder**

## The Query Builder interface

BIP offers you a very powerful tool for building your query.

On the left side of the window, as you can see in the following screenshot, you have a list of available tables in the mentioned **Catalog** and **Schema** of your database. You can simply click the desired table name and you'll have the table structure shown in the main section of the Query Builder interface. The four tabs provide different tools to fine tune your query:

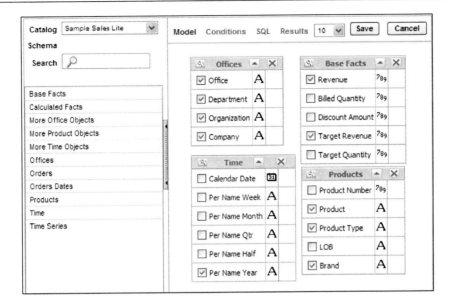

- **Model**: To check the fields and create links between the tables. The links between tables are created by simply dragging and dropping one table field over another, as shown in the preceding screenshot.

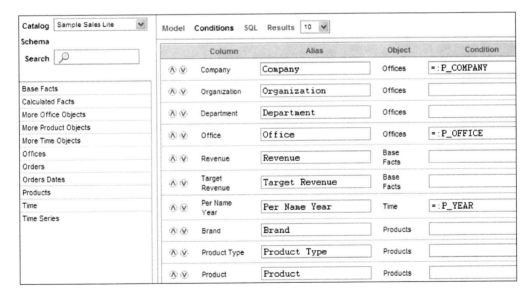

- **Conditions**: Enables filtering, ordering, sorting, grouping, calculations, entering field aliases, and so on, which is shown in the preceding screenshot.

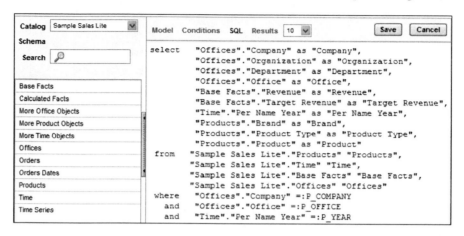

- **SQL**: All the options entered in the **Conditions** tab are gathered and as a result you have this SQL query – the third tab in the preceding screenshot.

- **Results:** The actual interrogation of the database is made and the **Results** tab displays the selected range of results – the fourth tab in the previous screenshot.

# Oracle BI analysis

The Oracle BI Presentation catalog is accessed through this type of data source and you can select an Oracle BI analysis as a data source.

 Integration with Oracle BI must be enabled.

To add the data set type of Oracle BI analysis to your Data Model, you must provide the following information as shown in the next screenshot:

- **Name**: The data set name
- **Oracle BI Analysis**: It can be used as the default name, selected from the Oracle BI presentation catalog
- **Time Out**: This is the time period in seconds that BIP waits for the analysis data and it is optional

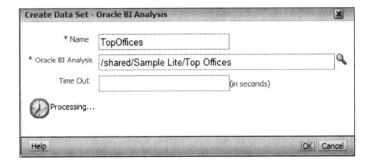

# XML file

In case of an XML file, you must select the XML filename. The next screenshot shows the information that you must provide:

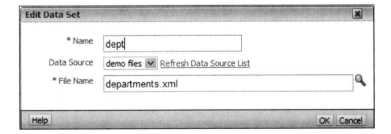

# Microsoft Excel file

To use an Excel file as a data set, you must first name your data. Use the Excel option **Define Name** as shown in the following screenshot:

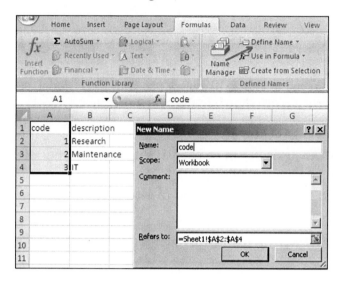

Once this step is completed, the data set can be created. You must provide the following information as shown in the following screenshot:

- **Table Name** specifies the table name used in case of multiple tables per sheet
- **Parameters** can be added from the report's list of parameters. Only one value per parameter is supported

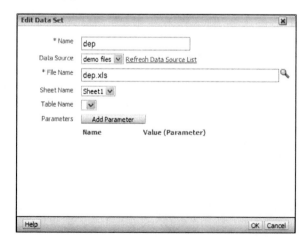

In this way, you will have the desired XLS structure translated into BIP.

# Data Structure builder

In order to provide an intuitive, well designed Data Model, its structure plays a very important role.

Improving your Data Model structure will result in easy-to-design and faster-running reports.

To build a data set's structure, the BIP's model editor offers you multiple views:

- Diagram view
- Structure view
- Code view

Let's now look at each of these in a bit more detail:

# Diagram view

As the following screenshot shows, the Data Model Editor allows you to:

- Create links between data from different data sets
- Create groups that can be used to separate data into sets or to filter data
- Aggregate data to apply aggregate functions on data elements
- Perform calculations to compute data values from multiple data elements

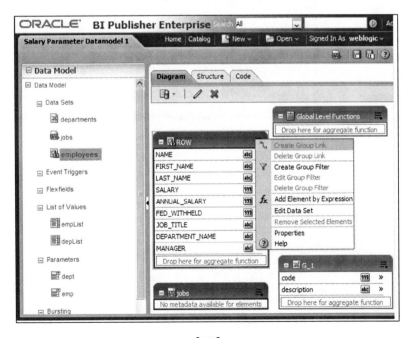

# Structure view

The Structure view has two models: **Table View** and **Output**.

While the Output model provides a non-updatable tree-like view of the data structure, the **Table View** allows you to update the XML element alias names, display names, null values, sorting, and reset options.

The **Table View** model is shown in the following screenshot:

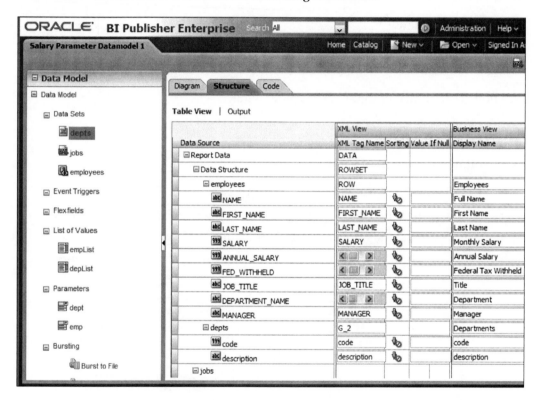

The **Output** model is shown in the following screenshot:

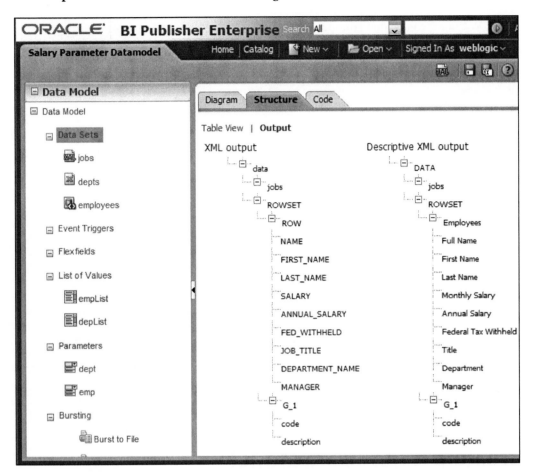

# Code view

Those familiar with the BIP 10g data template structure may remember that it includes a data structure section. As you can see in the following screenshot, the **Code** view shows a similar structure of elements: a dataStructure element containing many group and element tags. As data structure can now be considered an independent entity, we can see in the **Code** view that no other report-related entities are included or mentioned in its structure, as was the case for the data template:

The **Code** view is shown in the following screenshot:

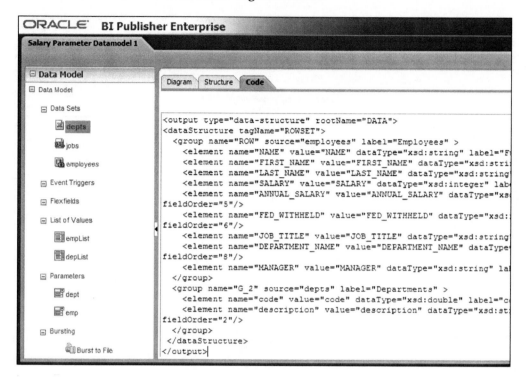

Let's start building a data structure in BIP's Data Model Editor using the previously described types.

# Creating a new Data Model

To create a new Data Model do the following:

- In the **Home** page choose **Data Model** to create a new Data Model, as shown in the following screenshot:

- The Data Model Editor interface opens, starting with the **Properties** page. Choose **mystore** as the **Default Data Source**, as shown in the following screenshot:

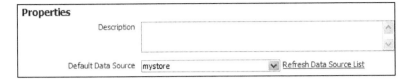

- On the left side of the page, click the **Data Sets** link. As you can see in the following screenshot, now you can choose your data set type. Choose **SQL Query**:

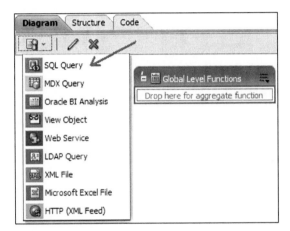

- For this data set you have to enter the following details as shown in the following screenshot:

    ◦ **Name**: The name of the data set displayed in the **Diagram** interface

    ◦ **Data Source**: Choose **mystore**, as this is the data source created for these examples, providing access to the Microsoft SQL database named MYSTORE

Now, let's continue with the Query Builder to build the query structure.

# Building the query structure

To build a query structure follow the steps given here:

1.  Choose the **Catalog** name (**MYSTORE**) and the **Schema** name (**dbo**). Enter a **Search** criteria to narrow your search area and get a smaller list of the available objects.

    As the following screenshot shows, on the left we have the filtered list of available tables:

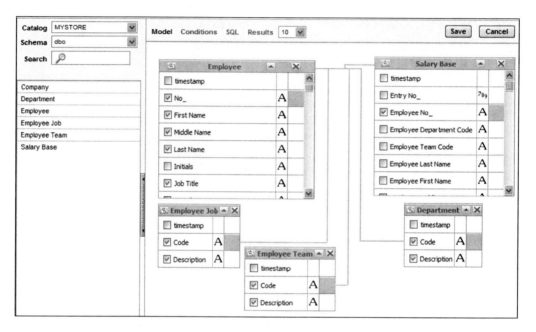

2.  In the **Model** tab, check the fields you want for your Data Model as shown in the preceding screenshot. For example, from the **Employee** table choose:
    - **No_**
    - **First Name**
    - **Middle Name**
    - **Last Name**
    - **Job Title**

3.  Create links between the tables. For example, **No_** from the Employee table has to be linked with the **Employee No_** field in the Salary Base table to obtain the desired result, that is, the employee and its salary in a row, as shown in the following screenshot.

4. Use the **Conditions** tab to change **Alias** column, to sort, group, filter, or calculate your data:

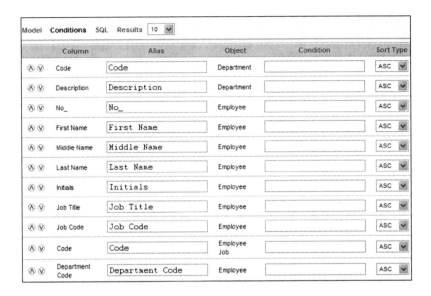

You will have your resulting SQL Query in the **SQL** tab, as you can see in the following screenshot:

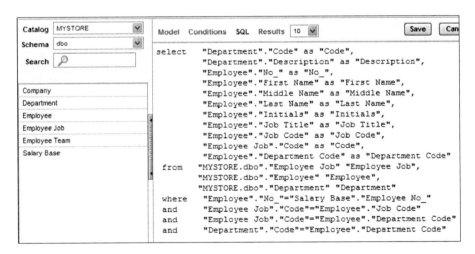

5. Don't forget to save your query.

# Data modelling using the Data Model Editor

Once the query is built and the data is available for further modelling, there are some actions that you can perform on this data, which are as follows:

1. Right-click on the group and choose **Add Element by Expressions** to create new calculated elements.

   If the necessary data is not available, new data fields can be calculated using data from the existing fields and operators as you can see in the following screenshot. **Add Element by Expressions** offers an expression builder interface and a tool: **Validate Expression**.

2. Calculate a new element called **NAME** by applying the concat function on the FIRST_NAME and the LAST_NAME fields.

 This is the list of all the available functions: MAX, MIN, ROUND, FLOOR, CEILING, ABS, AVG, LENGTH, SUM, NVL, CONCAT, STRING, SUBSTRING, INSTR, DATE, FORMAT_DATE, FORMAT_NUMBER, AND NUMBER.

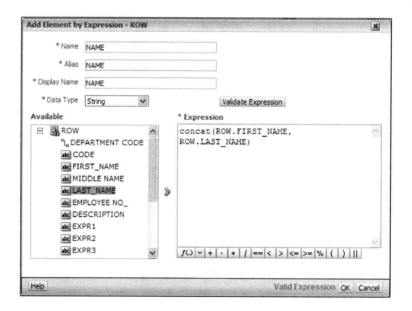

Another important tool offered is for grouping elements in the same data set by other elements. Our data set contains the DEPARTMENT_CODE field, which has the same value for employees from the same department.

3. Choose the **Group By** menu option as the following screenshot shows, and you'll have your employees grouped by departments:

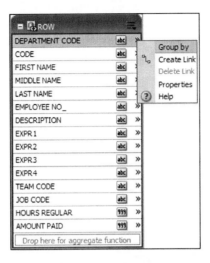

4. You can create links between two data sets.

Choose the **Create Link** option and the **Create** dialog will launch, displaying available elements to link your current element with.

In the following example, the **DEPARTMENT CODE** column from the **ROW** group is linked to the **CODE** column from the **G_2** group:

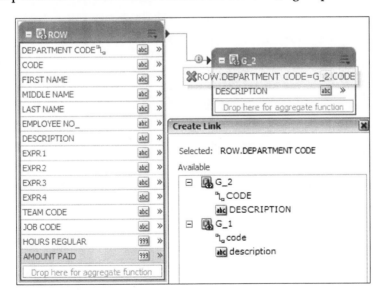

Once a parent-child link is created at the parent level, an aggregate element data can be created.

5. Drag the **AMOUNT PAID** element from the **G_2** (employees) over **G_1** (departments). The element named CS_1 is created, and as you can see in the following screenshot, you can choose any of the following aggregate functions to apply:

   ○ **Count**
   ○ **Average**
   ○ **First**
   ○ **Last**
   ○ **Maximum**
   ○ **Minimum**
   ○ **Summary**

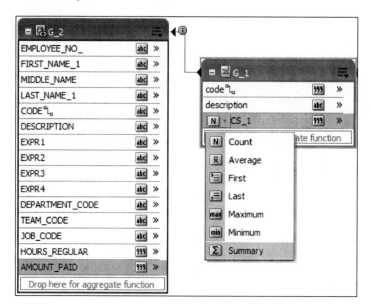

6. Use the **Structure** view to manage the element's **Business View**.

7.  Change the element's CS_1 **Display Name** into AMOUNT_PAID, as this will be the name displayed by the reports using this Data Model, as shown in the following screenshot:

| Data Source | XML View | | | Business View |
|---|---|---|---|---|
| | XML Tag Name | Sorting | Value If Null | Display Name |
| Report Data | DATA | | | |
| Data Structure | ROWSET | | | |
| departments | G_1 | | | G_1 |
| code | code | | | code |
| description | description | | | description |
| G_2.AMOUNT_PAID | AMOUNT_PAID | | | AMOUNT PAID |
| employee | G_2 | | | G_2 |
| DEPARTMENT CODE | DEPARTMENT_CODE | | | DEPARTMENT CODE |
| employee | G_3 | | | G_3 |
| EMPLOYEE NO_ | EMPLOYEE_NO_ | | | EMPLOYEE NO_ |

# Getting XML output

To test your data, use the **Get XML output** option. It will display a page as the following screenshot shows. On this page, you must select the **Number of rows to return** and enter the desired values for parameters.

As an example, let's choose **50** rows to return and **All** as the **Department parameter**:

Click **Run** and you will have your data displayed. Now you have the option to save your data as sample data or to export the XML for later use at the report's layout template design. Both actions are available by clicking the **Option** toolbar button.

# Event triggers

**Event triggers** are the equivalent of Report triggers from the Data Template in BIP 10g. A trigger can be set to fire before or after the completion of the report. This will call one or more database functions. To get access to these functions, an Oracle DB Default Package has to be mentioned on the Data Model Properties interface:

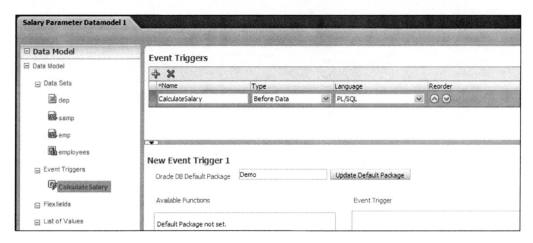

As you can see in the preceding screenshot, you can change the default package. Once the package is set, a list of **Available Functions** is displayed and you can add one or more functions to the **Event Trigger** list using this interface. For example, salary calculation is too complicated to be included in a report expression, so we can move it out in a database package.

# Flexfields

**Oracle flexfield** is an important feature of the Oracle Applications tool. It is because of the flexfields that Oracle Applications is so generic in nature and can be used to suit any industry or organization. Being so important for Oracle Applications, flexfields also needs to be integrated with BIP.

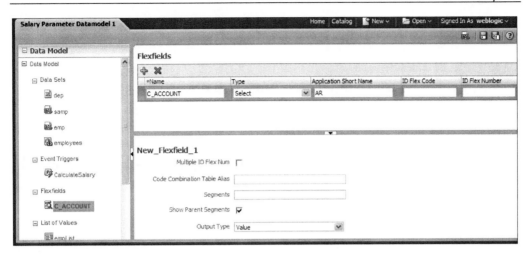

To add a flexfield to your Data Model, enter the following details as shown in the preceding screenshot:

- **Name**: The name of your flexfield component.
- **Type:** Choose a type from **Segment Metadata**, **Select**, **Where**, **Order By**, and **Filter**. Depending on the type you choose, a specific list of more detailed characteristics appears at the end of the flexfield table.
- **Application Short Name**: This can be an abbreviation for the name of the flexfield, for example, GL.
- **ID Flex code**: The code defined in the Register Key flexfield is the code for this flexfield.
- **ID Flex Number**: The name of the source column or parameter that contains the flexfield structure information.

# List of Values

You can add two types of **List of Values (LOVs)** to a Data Model: SQL Query or Fixed Data.

For the SQL type, as you can see in the following screenshot, you must do the following:

- Select a **Data Source**
- Check **Cache Result** if you want your result to be cached for the current session
- Enter or build your **SQL Query**

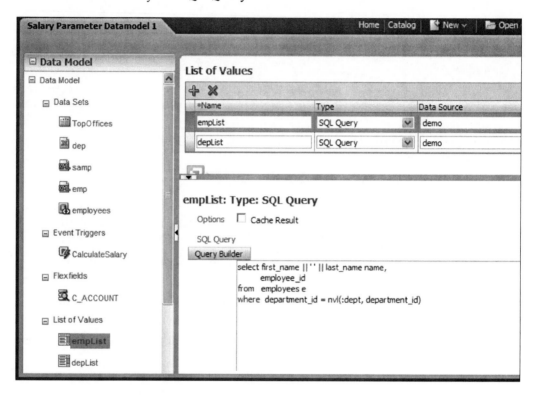

The other type, **Fixed Data** requires pairs Label, that is the value to be entered.

# Parameters

The available types of parameters are: **Text**, **Menu**, and **Date**.

You can see in the following screenshot that type menu uses the LOV already defined previously:

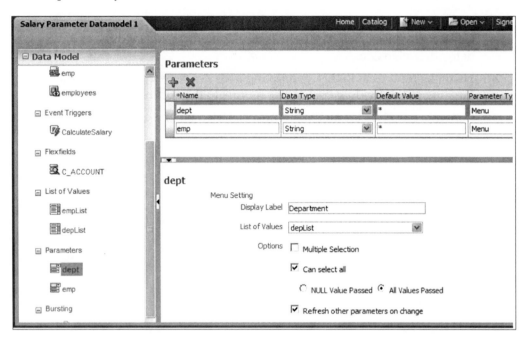

A menu type parameter also needs the following settings:

- **Display Label**: The Parameter's description displayed at runtime
- **Options**: There are three options provided:
    ◦ **Multiple Selection**: Allows you to select more than one value from the list
    ◦ **Can select all**: Includes an All option in the list and when this value is selected you can choose to pass null values or all values
    ◦ **Refresh other parameters on change**: Performs a page refresh, taking into consideration all the values linked to the current value

# Bursting

You can use bursting options when you need your reports to be delivered to different destinations in different formats.

Here are some examples of circumstances in which using bursting would be a good choice:

- Generate invoices, delivery based on customer-specific layouts, and delivery preference
- Financial reporting, that is, generating a master report of all cost centers and bursting out individual cost center reports to the appropriate manager
- Generate pay slips for all the employees based on one extract and deliver via e-mail

The possible output types are:

- HTML
- PDFZ (zipped PDF)
- PDF
- RTF
- EXCEL
- EXCEL2000
- MHTML
- PPT
- PPTX
- XSLFO
- XML
- CSV
- ETEXT

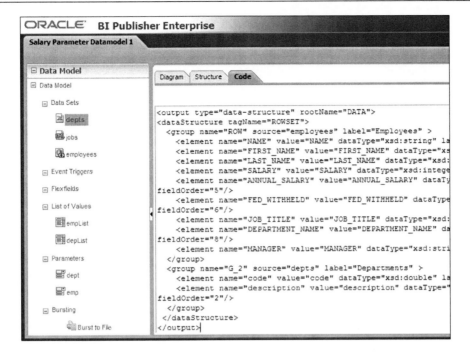

For a bursting definition, as you can see in the preceding screenshot, you must provide:

- **Name**: Enter a description of your choice
- **Type**: The only type available for a bursting definition is SQL Query
- **Data Source**: The data source containing delivery information
- **Split By**: An element from the data; data set must be ordered or sorted by this element
- **Deliver By**: Defines how delivery data and formats are applied
- **SQL Query**: The query containing formatting and delivery details

# Summary

After completing our walk through the Data Model Editor universe, I hope you realise what a complex and powerful tool it is. The variety of tools and features offered allow you to create data structures that enable optimal document generation.

In the next chapter, we will see even more complex Data Model examples using multiple data sources.

# 3
# Multiple Data Sources

We met the Data Model Editor in the previous chapter. The editor's interface deals with all the components and functionalities needed for the data model to achieve the structure you need. However, the main component is **Data Set**. In BIP, to create your data model structure you can choose from a variety of data set types:

- SQL Query
- MDX Query
- Oracle BI Analysis
- View Object
- Web Service
- LDAP Query
- XML file
- Microsoft Excel file
- Oracle BI Discoverer
- HTTP

Taking advantage of this variety requires multiple **Data Sources** of different types to be defined in the BIP. In this chapter, we will see:

- How data sources are configured
- How the data is retrieved from different data sets
- How data set type characteristics and the links between elements influence the data model structure

# Administration

Let's first see, how you can verify or configure your data sources. You must choose the **Administration** link found in the upper-right corner of any of the BIP interface pages, as shown in the following screenshot:

The connection to your database can be chosen from the following connection types:

- Java Database Connectivity (JDBC)
- Java Naming and Directory Interface (JNDI)
- Lightweight Directory Access Protocol (LDAP)
- Online Analytical Processing (OLAP)

# Available Data Sources

To get to your data source, BIP offers two possibilities:

1. You can use a **connection**. In order to use a connection, these are the available connection types:
   - JDBC
   - JNDI
   - LDAP
   - OLAP

2. You can also use a **file**.

In the following sections, the Data Source types — JDBC, JNDI, OLAP Connections, and File — will be explained in detail.

# JDBC Connection

Let's take the first example. To configure a Data Source to use JDBC, from the **Administration** page, choose **JDBC Connection** from the **Data Sources** types list, as shown in the following screenshot:

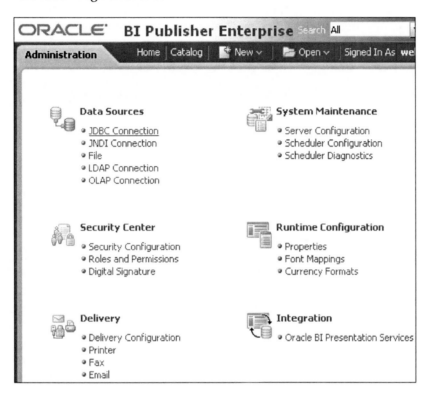

You can see the requested parameters for configuring a JDBC connection in the following screenshot:

- **Data Source Name**: Enter a name of your choice.
- **Driver Type**: Choose a type from the list. The relating parameters are:
    - ○ **Database Driver Class**: A driver, matching your database type.
    - ○ **Connection String**: Information containing the computer name on which your database server is running, for example, port, database name, and so on.
- **Username**: Enter a database username.
- **Password**: Provide the database user's password.

The **Use System User** option allows you to use the operating system's credentials as your credentials. For example, in this case, your MS SQL Database Server uses Windows authentication as the only authentication method.

When you have a system administrator in-charge of these configurations, all you have to do is to find which are the available Data Sources and eventually you can check if the connection works. Click on the **Test Connection** button at the bottom of the page to test the connection:

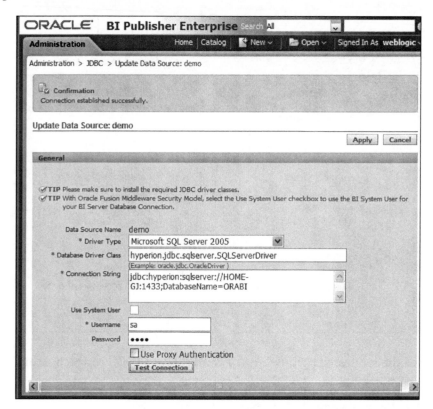

# JNDI Connection

JNDI Connection pool is in fact another way to access your JDBC Data Sources. Using a connection pool increases efficiency by maintaining a cache of physical connections that can be reused, allowing multiple clients to share a small number of physical connections.

In order to configure a Data Source to use JNDI, from the **Administration** page, choose **JNDI Connection** from the **Data Sources** types list. The following screen will appear:

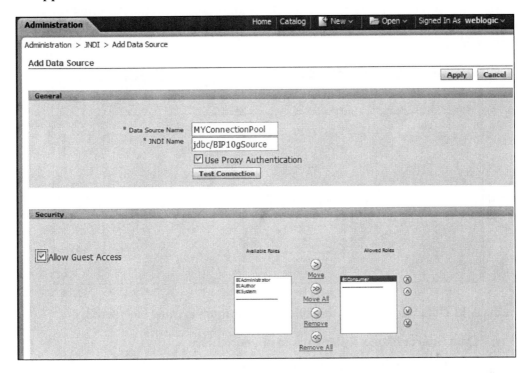

As you can see in the preceding screenshot, on the **Add Data Source** page you must enter the following parameters:

- **Data Source Name**: Enter a name of your choice
- **JNDI Name**: This is the JNDI location for the pool set up in your application server, for example, **jdbc/BIP10gSource**

The users having roles included in the **Allowed Roles** list only will be able to create reports using this Data Source.

# OLAP Connection

Use the OLAP Connection to connect to OLAP databases. BI Publisher supports the following OLAP types:

- Oracle Hyperion Essbase
- Microsoft SQL Server 2000 Analysis Services

- Microsoft SQL Server 2005 Analysis Services
- SAP BW

In order to configure a connection to an OLAP database, from the **Administration** page, choose **OLAP Connection** from the **Data Sources** types list. The following screen will appear:

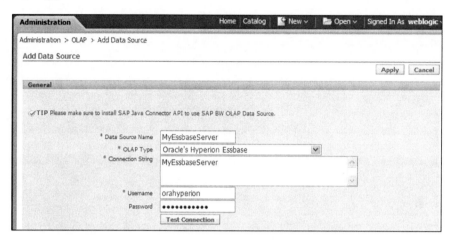

On the **Add Data Source** page, the following parameters must be entered:

- **Data Source Name**: Enter a name of your choice
- **OLAP Type**: Choose a type from the list
- **Connection String**: Depending on the supported OLAP databases, the connection string format is as follows:
  - Oracle Hyperion Essbase

Format: [server name]

  - Microsoft SQL Server 2000 Analysis Services

Format: Data Source=[server];Provider=msolap;Initial Catalog=[catalog]

  - Microsoft SQL Server 2005 Analysis Services

Format: Data Source=[server];Provider=msolap.3;Initial Catalog=[catalog]

  - SAP BW

Format: ASHOST=[server] SYSNR=[system number] CLIENT=[client] LANG=[language]

- **Username** and **Password**: Used for OLAP database authentication

# File

Another example of a data source type is **File**. In order to gain access to XML or Excel files, you need a File Data Source. In order to set up this kind of Data Source, only one step is required—enter the path to the **Directory** in which your files reside. You can see in the following screenshot that **demo files** Data Source points to the default BIP files directory. The file needs to be accessible from the BI Server (not on your local machine):

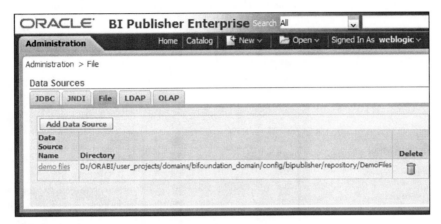

# Multiple Data Sources

Having a large amount of data at your disposal for creating a Data Source necessitates a great effort in creating a good structure of data with the necessary relationships between its elements.

Here are some of the tools, provided by BIP 11g Data Model Editor to design links between elements in your Data Model structure.

# Add different types of Data Sets to a Data Model

You will see how the structure of the Data Model changes, after different data connections (links) are created.

As shown in the following screenshot, the Data Sets added are:

- **Independent**: An HTTP type Data Set
- **trend**: An Oracle BI Analysis type Data Set

- **Sales**: A XML file type Data Set
- **countries**: A Microsoft Excel file type Data Set
- **reader**, **library**, and **book**: SQL Query type Data Sets

No links between the inserted Data Sets are created at this moment.

 From the XML file and HTTP Data Sets, no metadata is available, hence you cannot create links using these types of Data Set.

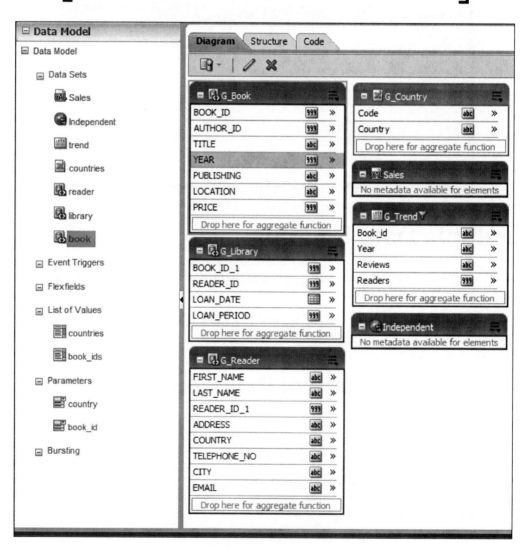

In the following screenshot, you can see from the **Structure** view that there is no hierarchy in the **Data Model**:

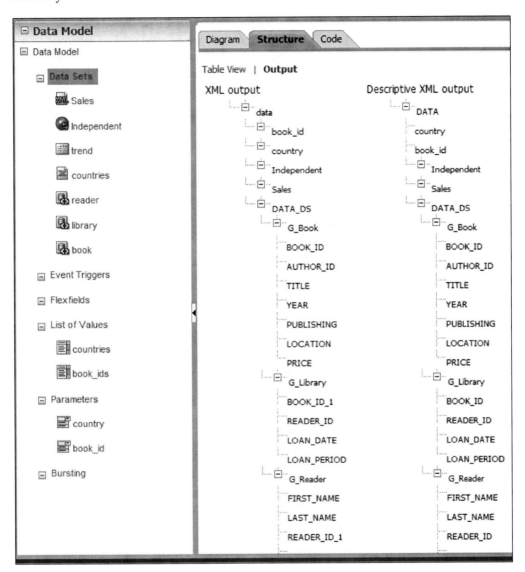

# Joins between Data Set objects

Using the Query Builder, you can create links between table columns as shown in the following screenshot. This kind of relationship is called a **join** and specifies how the rows of one table are combined with the rows of the second table. Columns of a table, view, or materialized view can be used to create links. Query Builder supports inner, outer, left, and right joins. You can find a detailed description of these operations in the **Structured Query Language (SQL)** documentation:

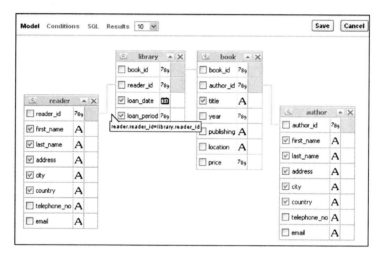

In the **SQL** tab of the Query Designer, you can see the SQL syntax generated for the created links. Three conditions were generated in a `where` clause. This is shown in the following screenshot:

```
Model    Conditions    SQL    Results    10

select    "reader"."last_name" as "reader_last_name",
          "reader"."first_name" as "reader_first_name",
          "reader"."address" as "reader_address",
          "reader"."city" as "reader_city",
          "reader"."country" as "reader_country",
          "library"."loan_date" as "loan_date",
          "library"."loan_period" as "loan_period",
          "book"."title" as "title",
          "author"."country" as "author_country",
          "author"."city" as "author_city",
          "author"."address" as "author_address",
          "author"."last_name" as "author_last_name",
          "author"."first_name" as "author_first_name"
from      "dbo"."reader" "reader",
          "dbo"."library" "library",
          "dbo"."author" "author",
          "dbo"."book" "book"
where     "reader"."reader_id"="library"."reader_id"
and       "library"."book_id"="book"."book_id"
and       "author"."author_id"="book"."author_id"
```

*Chapter 3*

# Links between Data Sets

There are two options when creating Data Sets links. You can create element-level or group-level links.

## Element-level links

An **Element-level link** refers to a link created between an element of a Data Set and an element of another Data Set. In this way, a parent-child relationship is created between different Data Sets.

As the following screenshot shows, by binding the **READER_ID** column from the **G_Library** group and the **READER_ID_1** column from the **G_Reader** group, a link was created between the two mentioned groups:

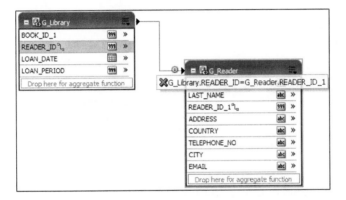

You can link different types of Data Sets using element-level links. The procedure for creating a link has been covered in the previous chapter. For example, as you can see in the following screenshot, a link between a SQL Query Data Set and a Microsoft Excel file Data Set was created by dragging the parent field **Country** from the **G_Reader** group over the **Code** field in the **G_Country** child group:

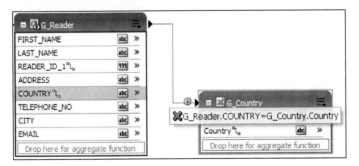

**[ 73 ]**

# Group-level links

A **group-level link** also defines a link between two Data Sets to obtain a hierarchically-structured XML. But in this case, the child group must have the same Data Set type as the parent group. For example, you cannot create a group-level link between **G_Reader** and **G_Country** (from the preceding screenshot), as one is a SQL Query Data Source type and the other is an MS Excel type.

To create a group-level link, go to the group menu (upper-right corner of the group) and choose the **Create Group Link** option. The following screenshot shows, how available **Child Groups** are displayed for selection when a **Group link** is created:

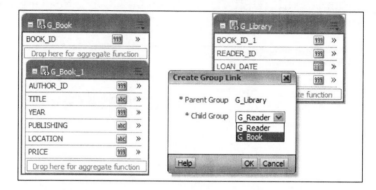

There is another request for a group-level link to work. You have to define a bind variable in the child query, as shown in the following screenshot. This variable is linked to a column from the parent Data Set.

Considering **G_Book** (the child group), you can see that only the **Book_ID** field could be used as a link between **G_Library** and **G_Book,** as **Book_ID** is the only field which is common to both the groups:

 Group-level links are provided for backward compatibility with Data Templates from earlier versions of BIP. However, element-level links are preferred.

# Group-level aggregate elements

Once a parent-child link is created between two Data Sets, you can insert values obtained by applying aggregate functions on the child's elements into the parent data set. Depending on the element type, different aggregation functions are available. As you can see in the following screenshot, for a string data type element, you can choose between the following functions:

- **COUNT**
- **FIRST**
- **LAST**

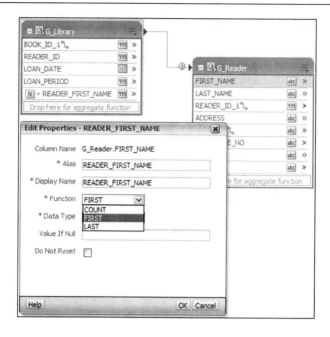

# Global-level functions

There is a special group in the Data Model designer: **Global Level Functions**, and you can add values to this group, obtained by the aggregation of elements belonging to any of the available Data Sets. For example, let's add a value called **TOTAL_BOOKS** to the **Global Level Functions** group. To obtain this value, as the following screenshot reveals, the aggregation function **COUNT** is used on the **BOOK_ID** field from the **G_Book** group. The same procedure is used to obtain the values: **TOTAL_LOANS**, **TOTAL_READERS**, and **TOTAL_COUNTRIES**:

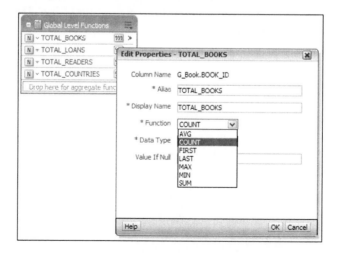

You can further refine the result and create more complicated expressions, such as the example shown in the following screenshot:

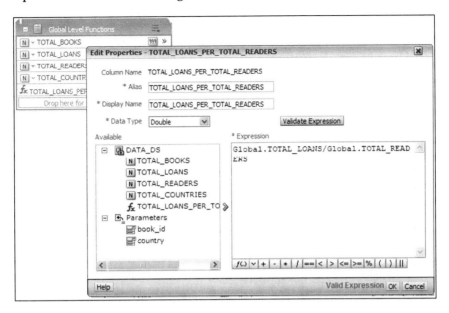

# Parameters

In order to add parameters to a data set, parameters must be first declared.

For example, let's add a **List of Values** (LOV) named **countries,** as shown in the following screenshot:

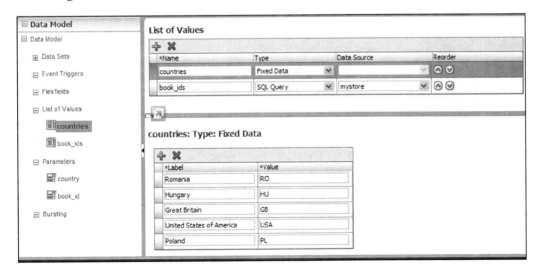

A parameter named **country** is defined and it uses the LOV **countries**, as shown in the following screenshot:

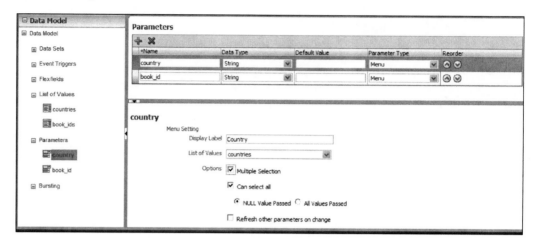

After a parameter is defined, there are many ways to use it. The advantage is more accurate and precise data for the reports using the parameterized data model.

# SQL Query statements

You can use parameters in **SQL Query** statements. For example, by including the parameter **country,** as shown in the following screenshot, the readers list is narrowed to the readers from a specific country:

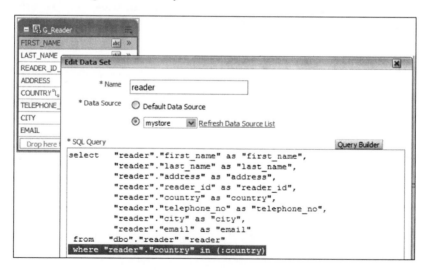

# Group filter expressions

Another option is to use parameters in group filter expressions. The result is similar to the previously described case, with the difference being that a group filter can also be used for another Data Set type than SQL type; for example, an Oracle BI Analysis Data Set (**G_Trend**) can be filtered using a parameter-based filter expression as you can see in the following screenshot:

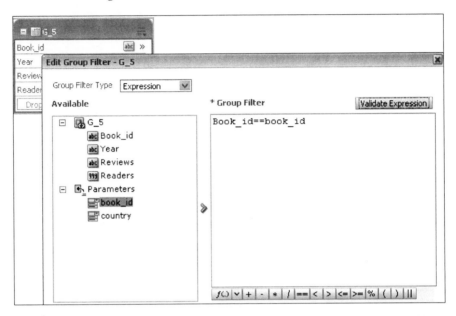

# Data Set parameters

You can also specify parameters when you create a Data Set. In the following screenshot, you can see the interface to add parameters to an HTTP Data Set:

The following screenshot shows the interface for a Microsoft Excel file data set type:

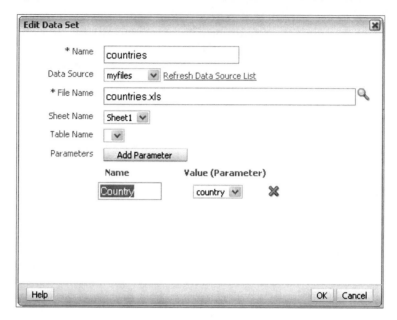

 Microsoft Excel Data Set types support only one value per parameter.

As opposed to HTTP and Microsoft Excel Data Set types, for an Oracle BI Analysis Data Set type, you cannot add parameters, as you can see in the following screenshot. Parameters and lists of values will be inherited from the BI analysis and they will show up at runtime:

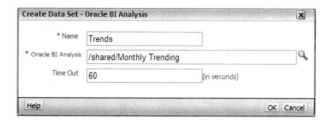

However, there are a few actions supported by this Data Set type:

- Global level functions
- Group filters
- Setting the value for elements in case of null values

Finally, the following screenshot shows, how the Data Model structure changed to reflect the links between Data Sets and group-level filters:

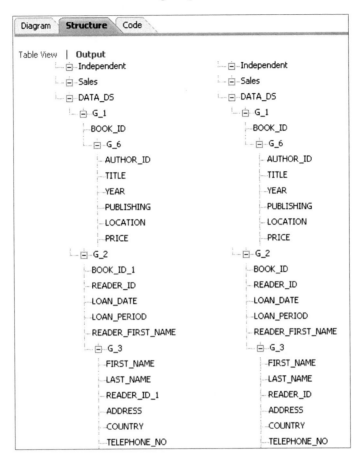

There are only a few cases in which Data Models with multiple Data Sources are recommended:

- When you need to perform functions not supported by the query type
- When the Data Model has to support complex views
- When you want to simulate a view, in case you don't have a view or you don't want to use one

Otherwise, it is recommended that the number of Data Sets used be reduced. The reason is that single Data Set models execute faster than multiple Data Set models—in a parent-child hierarchy the child is executed for each element of the parent. However, the main advantage of a Data Model based on multiple data sets remains, and thus, a model offers a more intuitive and simple view of the data structure.

# Summary

In this chapter, we saw how to use different tools offered by the Data Model Editor to shape a data structure composed of multiple data sets, into a compact and organized form.

For reports, the advantage of using a good structured Data Model is easy and also provides intuitive data access.

Keeping in mind the various aspects related to the Data Model structure we will proceed with the report layout design in the next chapter.

# Report Layout Template

When creating a report using Oracle BI Publisher 11g, the report has two main components—the Data Model and the Layout Template. In this chapter, we will see:

- How to add a layout to a report
- Which are the options available when choosing Layout Template types
- Output types for a report.

## Add a Report Layout Template

There are a few steps that you need to follow to add a Layout Template:

1. **Save the created Data Model**: After creating the Data Model structure for a report, it should be saved for further use in the report creation phase.

   As you can see in the following screenshot, a new object is added to the desired **Catalog** folder:

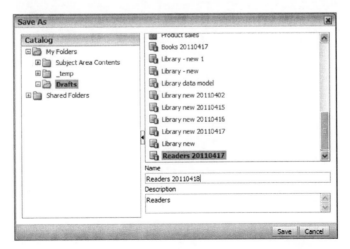

2. **Save a sample data**: Sample XML data is needed in the layout design phase. On the XML output page, choose **Save As Sample data**, as shown in the following screenshot. Try to save a small but representative set of data, because a small sample file will help in improving the performance when used in a layout design:

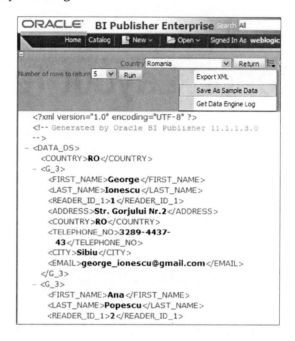

3. **Create a new report**: In order to create a new report, choose **Report** from the home page or from the menu, as shown in the following screenshot:

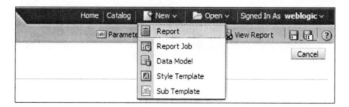

4. **Choose an existing Data Model**: For the newly created report, you will be asked to choose an existing Data Model. Browse to the desired saved Data Model and click on it, as shown in the following screenshot:

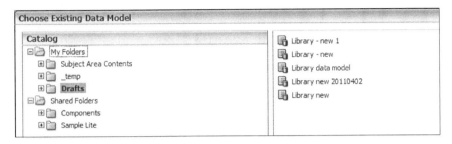

5. Finally, the **Create report interface** will be displayed. From this point, as you can see in the following screenshot, you have three options:

First, you can create a layout by choosing an option from the **Basic Templates** or **Shared Templates** section. A new layout will be created using BI Publisher's Layout Editor.

Second, you can upload a layout or you can choose to upload an existing layout, already created with an external tool. The **Upload or Generate Layout** section allows you to use the following template types:

- ○ RTF
- ○ PDF
- ○ Excel
- ○ Flash
- ○ XSL Stylesheet
- ○ eText

Finally, the third option allows you to generate a layout. Using this option, a RTF template can be automatically generated, which is shown in the following screenshot:.

 RTF Templates are generated using a standard format. You can start with this version in case you don't have your own standard layout format for the reports. When a distinct format is preferred, the better choice is to start with your personalized layout.

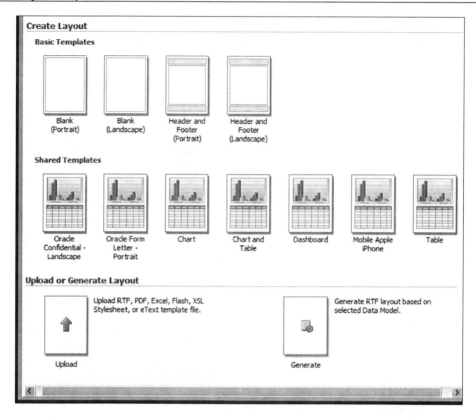

# Layout Template types

In order to help you to choose a Template type, here are a few characteristics of each type that you can use in BI Publisher 11g.

# BI Publisher Template

This is the new Layout Template introduced by BI Publisher 11g. It can generate reports in the following formats:

- PDF
- RTF
- Excel
- PowerPoint
- HTML

The most exciting feature of this Template type is the interactive HTML output that allows you to execute actions such as dynamic sorting, grouping, or filtering. It is recommended for simple to medium reports to get the best response times in case of the interactive output; however, its performance is similar to that of an RTF report when generating a static output.

In the following screenshot, you can see some of the components of the BI Publisher layout editor. On the left, the **Data Source** pane displays all your Data Model elements. You can drag the desired element and insert it into a layout component:

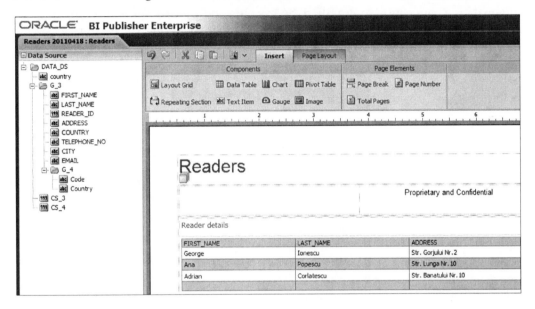

For layout and layout components manipulation, two toolbars are provided:

- The static toolbar for actions such as:
    - Undo or redo
    - Copy or paste
    - Layout preview
    - Layout create, open, and save

- The tabbed toolbar for actions such as:
    - Component insert
    - Page layout components
    - Component-specific actions (currently selected component)

The **design area** occupies the remaining space of the layout editor.

You will see a more detailed approach of the BI Publisher Template further in the next chapter.

# RTF Template

RTF Templates use **Rich Text Format (RTF)**, a specification used by common word processing applications, including Microsoft Word.

BIP provides a plugin—**Template Builder for Word**—that assists in template design and enables a connection to the BIP to access data and upload templates directly from Word. As shown in the following screenshot, you can find the necessary link for downloading this tool on the home page:

BIP supports Word format features, as well as advanced reporting features such as conditional formatting, dynamic data columns, running totals, and charts.

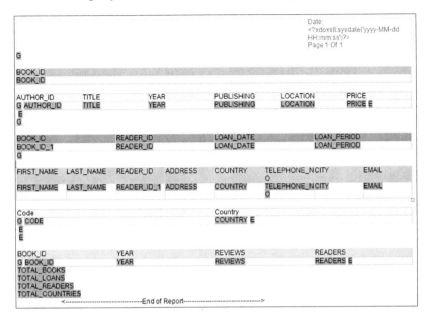

As you can see in the preceding screenshot, which shows the BIP generated RTF for the chosen Data Model, **Placeholders** and **Groups** are inserted for mapping data to the template. Placeholders are tags within a template that contain the name of a corresponding XML element. Groups contain processing instructions for BIP.

You can add data fields and other markups to your template, as shown in the following screenshot. BI Publisher's simplified tags for XSL expressions are used to make the task easy for you:

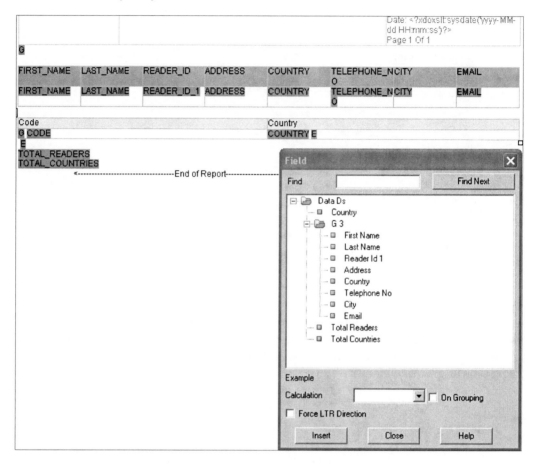

BI Publisher also supports the use of pure XSL elements in the template and you can use pure XSL/XSL:FO code instead of simplified tags.

Generated report types using RTF Templates are:

- PDF
- HTML
- Excel
- RTF
- Power Point

The **Preview** report function is provided by the BIP's plugin for Word, as you can see in the following screenshot:

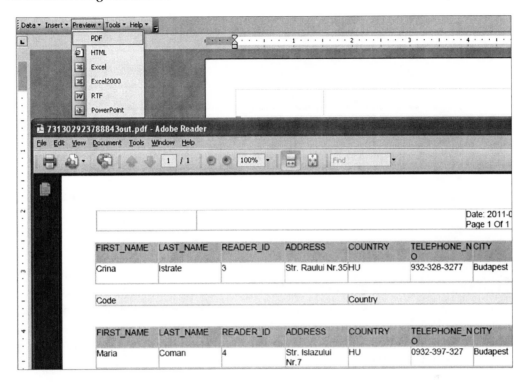

In this way, you do all the work required by the report design phase in Word and you instantly have access to the desired type of generated output, without even opening BIP.

In the following screenshot, you can see both the RTF tags and the generated PDF file.

After the report design phase is completed, you have to upload the template to BIP.

We will go into more details with this template type and the Template Builder for Word in *Chapter 6, Oracle BIP Template Builder for Microsoft Word*:

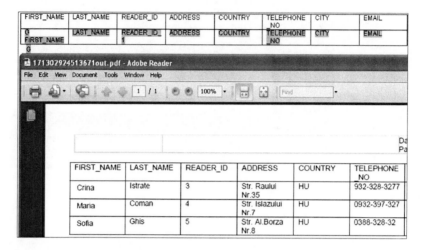

## Microsoft Excel Template

In order to design a Microsoft Excel Template, first you have to download and install **Analyzer for Excel**. As you can see in the following screenshot, from the home page, in the **Get Started** section, select **Analyzer for Excel** from the drop-down list. You can then proceed with the necessary steps:

There are two options available when working with the Excel analyzer:

- **Online mode**: In this case:
  - ° You have to enable macros
  - ° You can update report parameters or apply a new BIP template

- **Offline mode**: By choosing this option:
  - ° You can handle large Data Sets more efficiently
  - ° You can enable your own macros
  - ° You cannot login or connect to the BI Publisher server from the Microsoft Excel session

Here are the steps required when working with the Analyzer for Excel tool in online mode:

1. In the **Report Viewer** window, choose **Analyzer for Excel** from the menu, as shown in the following screenshot:

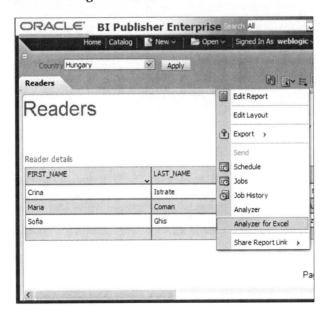

2. When prompted, click on the **Enable Macros** button as shown in the following screenshot:

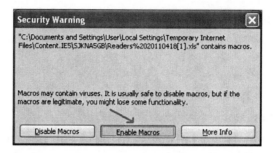

The report is displayed but currently does not contain any data.

3. Connect to Oracle BI Publisher using the **Login** option from the menu, as shown in the following screenshot:

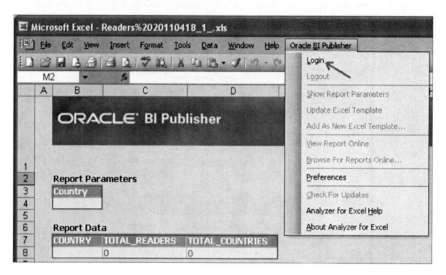

4. Choose the values of the desired report parameters and refresh data.

The report that we have here, has only one parameter named **Country**. After choosing a value for this parameter, you have to click on the **Refresh Data** menu action, as shown in the following screenshot, to get data from the saved XML sample file:

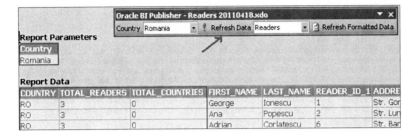

5. Apply a Layout Template and refresh the report.

   You must select a layout that allows HTML output. Let's choose the template named **Readers** as this is a BI Publisher Template. Now, click on **Refresh Formatted Data** and you will have the Readers Template applied. Also, data will be displayed according to the chosen template, as shown in the following screenshot:

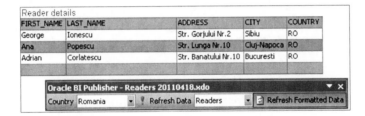

# XSL Stylesheet Template

In order to apply the XSL Stylesheet Template, select the **Export** option from the Template Builder for Word tools menu and then select **XSL-FO Stylesheet**, as shown in the following screenshot. This will export your RTF file in an XSL Stylesheet format:

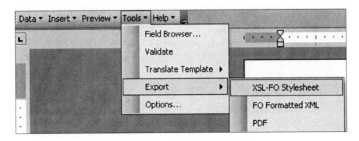

In the following screenshot, you can see a sequence from the generated XSL file:

```
-    <fo:table-cell padding-top="0.0pt" padding-bottom="0.0pt" border-end-width="0.5pt" border-end-style="solid" borde
     number-columns-spanned="1" padding-end="0.0pt" border-bottom="0.5pt solid #dddddd" border-start-width="0.5p
     height="0.0pt" background-color="#b9d1e3" border-start-color="#dddddd" vertical-align="top">
  -    <fo:block padding-top="0.0pt" padding-bottom="0.0pt" start-indent="0.0pt" text-align="start" end-indent="0.0p
       <fo:inline height="9.0pt" white-space-collapse="false" font-family="Arial" color="#000000" font-size="9.0pt
       </fo:block>
     </fo:table-cell>
  </fo:table-row>
-  <fo:table-row>
  -    <fo:table-cell padding-top="0.0pt" padding-bottom="0.0pt" border-end-width="0.5pt" border-end-style="solid" borde
       number-columns-spanned="1" padding-end="0.0pt" border-bottom="0.5pt solid #dddddd" border-start-width="0.5p
       height="0.0pt" background-color="#ffffff" border-start-color="#dddddd" vertical-align="top">
    -    <fo:block padding-top="0.0pt" padding-bottom="0.0pt" start-indent="0.0pt" height="0.0pt" text-align="start" en
         note="FIRST_NAME">
      -    <fo:inline height="9.0pt" white-space-collapse="false" font-family="Arial" color="#000000" font-size="9.0pt
           <xsl:value-of select="(.//FIRST_NAME)[1]" xdofo:field-name="FIRST_NAME"/>
           </fo:inline>
         </fo:block>
       </fo:table-cell>
  -    <fo:table-cell padding-top="0.0pt" padding-bottom="0.0pt" border-end-width="0.5pt" border-end-style="solid" borde
       number-columns-spanned="1" padding-end="0.0pt" border-bottom="0.5pt solid #dddddd" border-start-width="0.5p
       height="0.0pt" background-color="#ffffff" border-start-color="#dddddd" vertical-align="top">
    -    <fo:block padding-top="0.0pt" padding-bottom="0.0pt" start-indent="0.0pt" height="0.0pt" text-align="start" en
         note="LAST_NAME">
      -    <fo:inline height="9.0pt" white-space-collapse="false" font-family="Arial" color="#000000" font-size="9.0pt
           <xsl:value-of select="(.//LAST_NAME)[1]" xdofo:field-name="LAST_NAME"/>
           </fo:inline>
         </fo:block>
       </fo:table-cell>
  -    <fo:table-cell padding-top="0.0pt" padding-bottom="0.0pt" border-end-width="0.5pt" border-end-style="solid" borde
       number-columns-spanned="1" padding-end="0.0pt" border-bottom="0.5pt solid #dddddd" border-start-width="0.5p
       height="0.0pt" background-color="#ffffff" border-start-color="#dddddd" vertical-align="top">
    -    <fo:block padding-top="0.0pt" padding-bottom="0.0pt" start-indent="0.0pt" height="0.0pt" text-align="start" en
         note="READER_ID_1">
      -    <fo:inline height="9.0pt" white-space-collapse="false" font-family="Arial" color="#000000" font-size="9.0pt
           <xsl:value-of select="(.//READER_ID_1)[1]" xdofo:field-name="READER_ID_1"/>
           </fo:inline>
         </fo:block>
       </fo:table-cell>
```

Now, upload the template into BIP, as shown in the following screenshot:

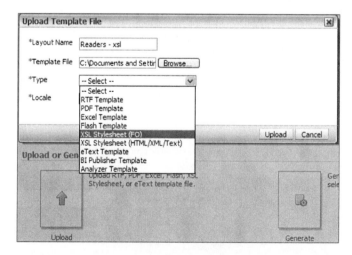

We saw that we can create an RTF template using BI Publisher's simplified syntax or we can generate an XSL-FO Stylesheet from the BIP's plugin for Word. However, you also have the option to use XSL or XSL-FO code instead of the simplified syntax. The following are the necessary steps required for adding components without using the Template Builder:

1. Let's take an XML file for example. The following screenshot shows this file:

```xml
<?xml version="1.0" encoding="UTF-8"?>
<!--Generated by Oracle BI Publisher 11.1.1.3.0-->
<DATA_DS>
    <COUNTRY>HU</COUNTRY>
  <LIST_G_READER>
    <READER>
        <FIRST_NAME>Crina</FIRST_NAME>
        <LAST_NAME>Istrate</LAST_NAME>
        <READER_ID_1>3</READER_ID_1>
        <ADDRESS>Str. Raului Nr.35</ADDRESS>
        <COUNTRY>HU</COUNTRY>
        <TELEPHONE_NO>932-328-3277</TELEPHONE_NO>
        <CITY>Budapest</CITY>
        <EMAIL>crina_istrate@yahoo.com</EMAIL>
    </READER>
    <READER>
        <FIRST_NAME>Maria</FIRST_NAME>
        <LAST_NAME>Coman</LAST_NAME>
        <READER_ID_1>4</READER_ID_1>
        <ADDRESS>Str. Islazului Nr.7</ADDRESS>
        <COUNTRY>HU</COUNTRY>
        <TELEPHONE_NO>0932-397-327</TELEPHONE_NO>
        <CITY>Budapest</CITY>
        <EMAIL>maria_coman@yahoo.com</EMAIL>
    </READER>
    <READER>
        <FIRST_NAME>Sofia</FIRST_NAME>
        <LAST_NAME>Ghis</LAST_NAME>
        <READER_ID_1>5</READER_ID_1>
        <ADDRESS>Str. Al.Borza Nr.8</ADDRESS>
        <COUNTRY>HU</COUNTRY>
        <TELEPHONE_NO>0388-328-32</TELEPHONE_NO>
        <CITY>Budapest</CITY>
        <EMAIL>sofia_chis@gmail.com</EMAIL>
    </READER>
  </LIST_G_READER>
    <TOTAL_READERS>3</TOTAL_READERS>
</DATA_DS>
```

Your template content has to follow the XML structure. Placeholders are defined for the XML elements and groups are defined for repeating elements.

2. To insert a placeholder in Microsoft Word 2010, go to **File** | **Options** | **Customize Ribbon**.

In the right pane, check **Developer** from the main tabs list to enable the **Form** toolbar, as shown in the following screenshot:

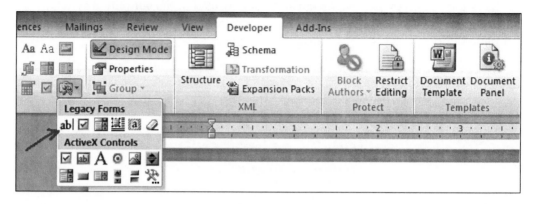

3. Insert a form field area in your document by selecting the **Text Form Field** icon as shown in the preceding screenshot.

4. In the **Text Form Field Options** dialog box (which is opened by double-clicking on the form field), enter a description for the field and the element's tag name in the **Help Text** field as the following screenshot shows:

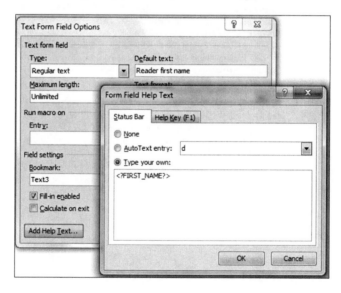

5. Create placeholders for each XML element. As the following screenshot shows, after completing the task, the template will look like this:

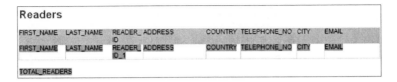

6. Create groups in the XML file. As you can see in the XML structure, **READER** is a repeating group. Thus, you have to insert form fields to mark the beginning and the end of a group:

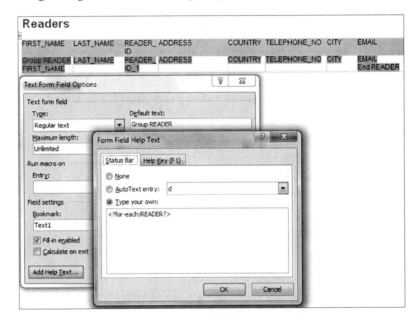

You have to use the following syntax in the **Help Text** field:

- `<?for-each: READER?>`: For the element inserted before the first element of the group
- `<?end for-each?>`: For the element inserted after the last element of the group

Notice the **Group READER** and **End READER** form fields inserted in the RTF document.

Let's now take a look at a more complex example to follow its code structure:

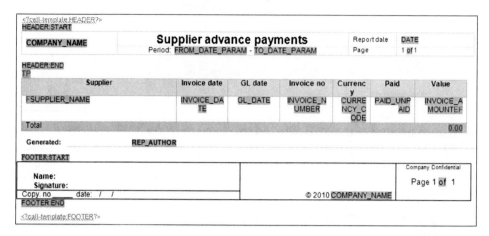

The following table shows the BI Publisher's simplified syntax. However, for using the form fields the procedure is the same as the procedure for XSL and FO elements:

| Text Field | Code |
|---|---|
| **HEADER:START** | `<?template:HEADER?>` |
| **COMPANY_NAME** | `<?COMPANY_NAME?>` |
| **DATE** | `<?xdoxslt:sysdate('dd.MM.YYYY HH24:mm:ss')?>` |
| **FROM_DATE_PARAM** | `<?FROM_DATE_PARAM?>` |
| **TO_DATE_PARAM** | `<?TO_DATE_PARAM?>` |
| **HEADER:END** | `<?end template?>` |
| **TP** | `<?xdoxslt:set_variable($_XDOCTX, 'TP', 0)?>` |
| **F** | `<?for-each:G_MAIN?> <?if:INVOICE_AMOUNT !=0?>` |
| **SUPPLIER_NAME** | `<?SUPPLIER_NAME?>` |
| **INVOICE_DATE** | `<?INVOICE_DATE?>` |
| **GL_DATE** | `<?GL_DATE?>` |
| **INVOICE_NUMBER** | `<?INVOICE_NUMBER?>` |
| **CURRENCY_CODE** | `<?CURRENCY_CODE?>` |
| **PAID_UNPAID** | `<?PAID_UNPAID?>` |
| **INVOICE_AMOUNT** | `<?INVOICE_AMOUNT?>` |

| Text Field | Code |
|---|---|
| E | `<?xdoxslt:set_variable($_XDOCTX, 'TP',`<br>`xdoxslt:get_variable($_XDOCTX, 'TP') + INVOICE_`<br>`AMOUNT)?><?end if?>` |
| F | `<?end for-each>` |
| 0.00 | `<?xdoxslt:get_variable($_XDOCTX, 'TP')?>` |
| REP_AUTHOR | `<?REP_AUTHOR?>` |
| FOOTER:START | `<?template:FOOTER?>` |
| COMPANY_NAME | `<?COMPANY_NAME?>` |
| FOOTER:END | `<?end template?>` |

# Other Template types

In order to give you a complete overview, let's take a look at the other accepted template types.

## PDF Template

PDF Templates are designed using Adobe Acrobat by applying a BI Publisher markup to an existing PDF document. You can use PDF files from any source, including downloaded predefined forms (such as government forms). There are a few requests concerning the tools you need:

- Adobe Acrobat Professional 5.0 or a later version to apply or edit PDF form fields
- Adobe Acrobat Distiller (optional) to convert Microsoft Word documents into PDF

In order to use form fields, you have to map Data Source element names to the PDF fields, to create placeholders for the data. You can define text, check box, or radio button placeholders.

BI Publisher supports the following options available from the **Text Field Properties** dialog box:

- **General**: This option provides the following settings:
    - Read Only
    - Required
    - Visible/Hidden
    - Orientation (degrees)

- **Appearance**: This option provides the following settings:
    - Border Settings (color, background, width, and style)
    - Text Settings (color, font, and size)
    - Border Style

- **Options tab**: You can set the following properties with this option:
    - Multi-line
    - Scrolling Text
- **Format tab**: This tab provides the settings for numbers
- **Calculate tab**: You can use the calculation functions provided in this tab

The following is a short insight of the syntax used:

- To define a group, enter `<?rep_field="T1_Gn"?>` (where n is the row number of the item on the layout) into the **Tooltip** field of **Text Field Properties** dialog.

    For text fields and checkboxes, the field name must match the name of the XML element.

- To add page breaks, enter `<?rep_field="T1_G1", page_break="yes"?>` into the **Tooltip** field.

PDF Templates are less flexible than RTF Templates, but more appropriate for creating form-like reports, such as invoices, purchase orders, and particularly those documents that do not require frequent updates.

# Flash Template

In order to work with PDF Templates, you need a few tools installed on your computer:

- Adobe Flash Player 9 — to view the report output from the Flash Template
- Adobe Flash Player 9 plugin — to view reports over the BIP user interface
- FlexBuilder IDE from Adobe — to build templates

I would recommend this template type for those who are already familiar with these technologies.

# eText Template

eText Templates are specialized RTF Templates for constructing **Electronic Funds Transfer** (EFT) and **Electronic Data Interchange** (EDI) transaction files. In other words, an EFT is an electronic transmission of financial data and payments to banks. EDI is a delimiter-based text file used to exchange business documents between companies.

The generated output text has a very specialized layout and BIP uses tables to define the position, length, value of the fields, and data manipulation commands. Each record is represented by a table.

The following screenshot shows an example of the instructions for filling an EFT file:

BATCH HEADER RECORD MODIFICATION REQUIREMENTS FOR LOUISIANA DEPARTMENT OF INSURANCE

| Field Name | Positions | Required Contents |
|---|---|---|
| Company Name | 05 - 40 | Enter the company name - up to 36 characters |
| Company Identification | 41 - 50 | Enter the number "1" plus the Federal Employer ID Number |
| Company Entry Description | 54 - 63 | Enter the NAIC Number (or Code) |

LOUISIANA DEPARTMENT OF INSURANCE
TAX PAYMENT (TXP) ADDENDA RECORD - ACH CREDIT
CCD + FORMAT

| Field Name Data Elements & Separators | Field Size | Position Start | Position End | Contents |
|---|---|---|---|---|
| Record Type Code | 1 | 01 | 01 | 7 |
| Addenda Type Code | 2 | 02 | 03 | 05 |
| Free Form Area | 80 | 04 | 83 | See Free Form Table Below |
| Special  Addenda Sequence Number | 4 | 84 | 87 | Refer to ACH Rules |
| Entry Detail Sequence Number | 7 | 88 | 94 | Refer to ACH Rules |

FREE FORM AREA

| Field Name Data Elements & Separators | Field Size | Position Start | Position End | Contents |
|---|---|---|---|---|
| Segment Identifier | 3 | 01 | 03 | TXP |
| Separator | 1 | 04 | 04 | * |
| NAIC Number (or Code) [1] | 5 to 7 | 05 | 11 | Numeric |
| Separator | 1 | 12 | 12 | * |
| Company Name | 36 | 13 | 48 | Text |
| Separator | 1 | 49 | 49 | * |
| Federal Employer Identification Number | 9 | 50 | 58 | Numeric |
| Separator | 1 | 59 | 59 | * |
| Payment Amount | 10 | 60 | 69 | $$$$$$$$¢¢ (include cents) |
| Separator | 1 | 73 | 73 | * |
| Tax/Fee Due Date | 6 | 74 | 79 | MMDDYY (numeric) |
| Terminator | 1 | 80 | 80 | \ fill to 80 with blanks [2] |

[1]  NAIC Number is the number issued to the company by the National Association of Insurance Commissioners or equivalent number issued by the Louisiana Department of Insurance.
[2]  Fill to position 80 with blanks after the terminator "\".

A sample EFT file generated considering these rules is shown in the following screenshot:

| Example | The addenda record for an annual license tax and/or fee payment of $11,323.85 due March 1, 2001 will appear as follows: |
|---|---|
| | TXP*12345*Shifting⊥Sand⊥Fire⊥Insurance⊥Company*123456789*1132385*030101\⊥⊥⊥⊥⊥ ⊥ = indicates a blank space |

As the use of this template type requires many specific commands and a lot of formatting, I won't go further describing all these specific features. You will have to do more extensive research before using it.

# Valid output types for layout types

The following table shows a list of output types, which you can get by choosing different layout types:

| Layout Type | Valid Output Types |
|---|---|
| PDF | PDF, PDFZ, CSV, Data |
| RTF | HTML, PDF, PDFZ, RTF, Excel, Excel2000, PowerPoint, PowerPoint2007, MHTML, CSV, FO, Data |
| XPT | Interactive, HTML, PDF, PDFZ, RTF, Excel, Excel2000, PowerPoint, PowerPoint2007, MHTML, CSV, FO, Data |
| XLS | Excel, Excel2000, CSV, Data |
| Flash | Flash, PDF, MHTML, CSV, Data |
| XSL Stylesheet (FO) | HTML, PDF, PDFZ, RTF, Excel, Excel2000, PowerPoint, PowerPoint2007, MHTML, CSV, FO, Data |
| XSL Stylesheet (HTML / XML / Text) | HTML, XML, Text, Data |
| eText | Text, CSV, Data |

# Summary

In this chapter, we saw a variety of Layout Template types that Oracle BI Publisher offers for designing your report. It is up to you to choose the tools that you prefer, but you also have to consider a few requests such as desired output type, interactivity, or performance.

In the following chapters, we will have a more detailed look at the BI Publisher Template type and the Template Builder for Word. After completing these, in the report configuration phase, you will know how to choose more suitable tools for your report.

# 5
# The New XPT Format

In the previous chapter, we learned about the types of Layout Templates that BIP offers for a report's design. The XPT format is a new template option and it is designed in a totally BIP-integrated layout design interface. In this chapter, we will see how to use this interface to design a complete report. We will cover the following topics in this chapter:

- The Layout Editor presentation
- Designing a Layout
- Export options

## The Layout Editor

First, you have to choose a predefined layout from the **Create Report Interface**. As you can see in the following screenshot, this interface displays a list of predefined layouts:

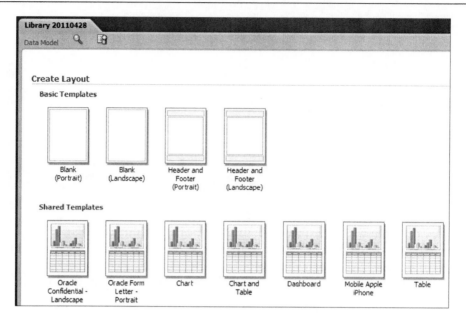

You can add your own predefined layouts to this list and make them available for your later use or even for all the users.

After choosing a layout from the **Basic Templates** or the **Shared Templates** group, the **Layout Editor interface** is displayed.

# Designing a Layout

In the Layout Editor Interface, as shown in the following screenshot, you have tools to perform activities such as:

- **Insert a component**: Select the desired component from the **Components** pane on the left or from the **Insert** tab of the toolbar and drag-and-drop it into the design area
- **Set component properties**: Set the component properties from the **Properties** pane on the left or from the component-specific tab of the toolbar (only the most commonly used components)

- **Insert a data element**: Drag the element from the **Data Source** pane to the design area

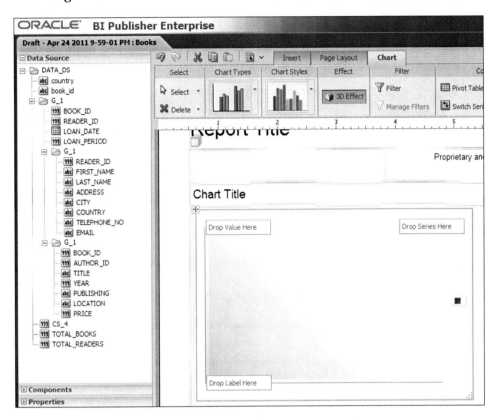

As shown in the preceding screenshot, a precise dropping area is marked. For example, in a chart you have the following marked areas:

- ◦ **Drop Value Here**
- ◦ **Drop Label Here**
- ◦ **Drop Series Here**

- **Set page layout options**: In order to set the page layout options, use the **Page Layout** tab and the **Properties** pane
- **Save the Layout**: Use the activity icons from the toolbar on the right side

In the following sections, a few elements will be inserted to complete our report design. You will also see the steps that you need to follow when inserting and setting the properties of these components.

# Text elements

In order to make changes in the settings of Text elements, follow the steps given here:

1. Click on the **Insert** tab and choose the **Text Item** component from the toolbar, as shown in the following screenshot:

2. Click on the **Text** tab and set a font color for your text using the **Font Color** icon from the toolbar, as shown in the following screenshot:

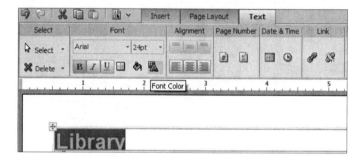

3. Set the text margins using the **Properties** panel, as shown in the following screenshot:

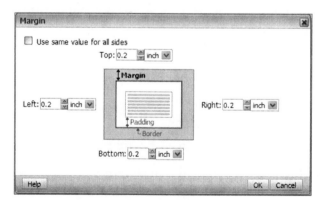

In this way, we obtain the desired report title, as you can see in the following screenshot:

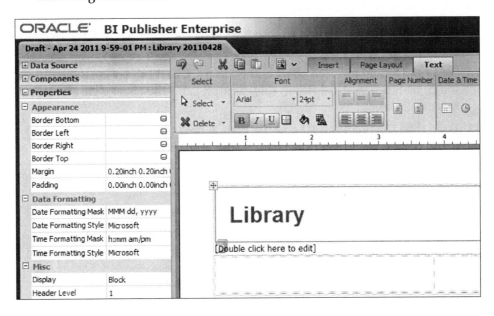

In order to insert data elements in our report's components, we will use the following Data Model:

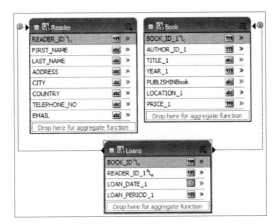

# Charts

In order to create Charts, follow the steps given here:

1. Click on the **Insert** tab and choose the **Chart** component from the toolbar, as shown in the following screenshot.

2. Select the newly inserted chart and go to the **Chart** tab on the toolbar to set the chart type (**Vertical Bar** in this example) and the chart style (**Project** in this example).

3. Drag the **LOAN_PERIOD** and the **PRICE** fields from the Data Source (from the left pane) over the **Drop Value Here** area of the design view.

4. Drop the **TITLE** field from the Data Source over the **Drop Label Here** area:

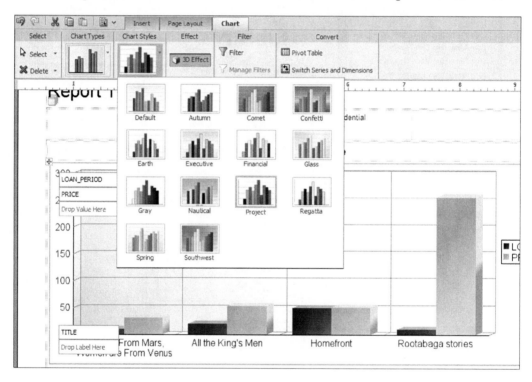

# Data tables

In order to create Data tables, follow the steps given here:

1. Click on the **Insert** tab and choose the **Data Table** component from the toolbar, as shown in the following screenshot.

2. Drag the fields **LOAN_DATE, LOAN_PERIOD, TITLE,** and **YEAR** from the Data Source over the area marked as **Drop a Data Item Here**.

3. Select the **LOAN_DATE** column and in the **Properties** pane set the **Formatting Mask** to **yyyy-mm-dd**.

4. For each column of the table, enter a suitable value for **Width**, in the **Properties** pane. For example, the first column has a width of 1.00 inch:

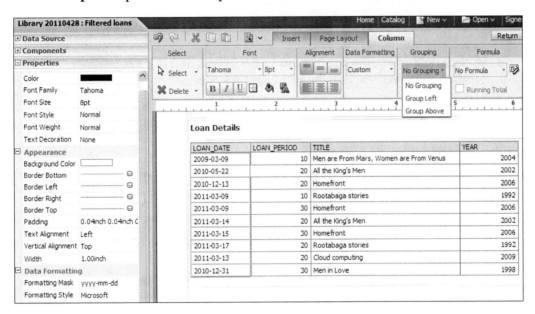

# Automatic filtering

Now, we will bring all the previously described components into a report, and create an interaction between the chart and the table. When viewing in an interactive mode, the events triggered by the user will determine the layout components to respond to these configured events.

For example, in order to filter the table rows according to the chart selection and to show only the selected section of the chart, follow the steps given here:

1. On the **Page Layout** tab of the toolbar, click on the **Configure Events** option. You will get the **Configure Events** interface.

2. Select **Chart 1** in the **Components** list. A list of events and a list of targets will be displayed, as shown in the following screenshot:

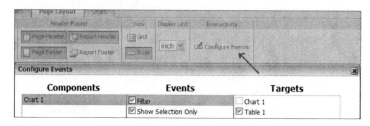

3. Check on the appropriate options in the **Events** and the **Targets** lists respectively, as shown in the preceding screenshot.

4. Click on the **Save** icon to save your layout.

5. Click on **Return** to see your result.

6. Click on a section of the chart.

As you can see in the following screenshot, only the selected section of the chart is displayed along with only those rows of the table that meet the selection criteria:

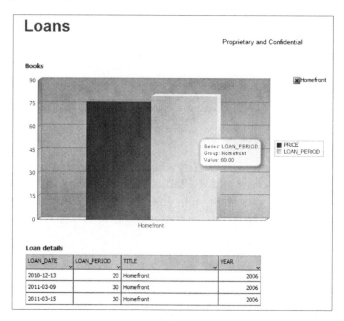

Notice that the data details are displayed when you mouseover a chart item.

Don't check the **Show Selection Only** option if you want to keep all the values of the chart and filter only the table values. The result will be as follows:

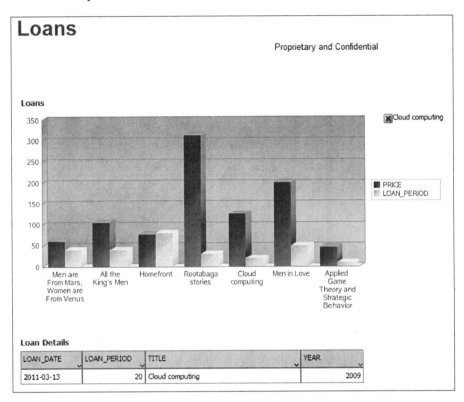

# Repeating sections

Repeating sections is used to group report data using a data element with multiple occurrences. In order to have all the loans of our example grouped by their titles, follow the steps given here:

1. Click on the **Insert** tab of the toolbar and choose **Repeating Section** to insert a Repeating Section, as shown in the following screenshot:

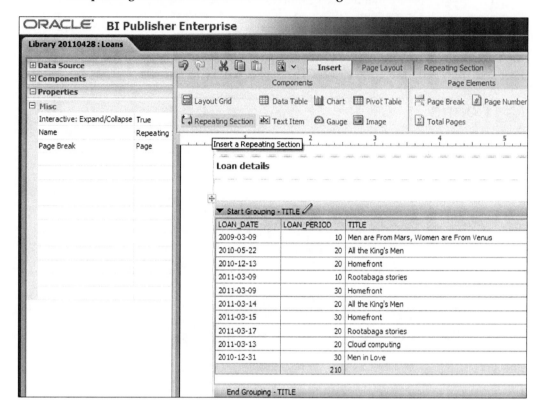

2. In the **Insert Repeating Section** dialog, enter **TITLE** as the repeating / grouping by element, as shown in the following screenshot:

 In case of nested sections, you can use **Group Detail** as the repeating / grouping by element.

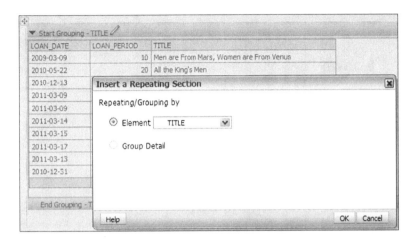

3. Save and return to check the elegant and interactive manner of BIP that displays repeating sections, as shown in the following screenshot:

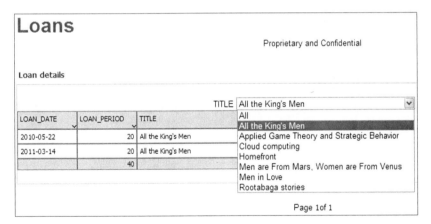

In order to see the difference, the same report is displayed in a PDF format, which is shown in the following screenshot. Seven groups are displayed following each other, or on different pages according to the page break option settings:

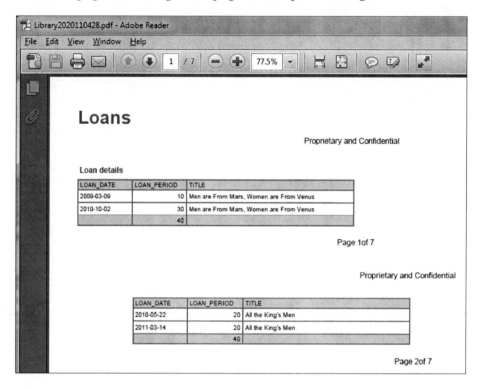

# Export options

Using your BIP Layout Template, you can generate reports in the following formats:

- PDF
- RTF
- Excel
- PowerPoint
- HTML

When viewing your report, click on **Actions** and then select **Export** to choose the desired export format, as shown in the following screenshot:

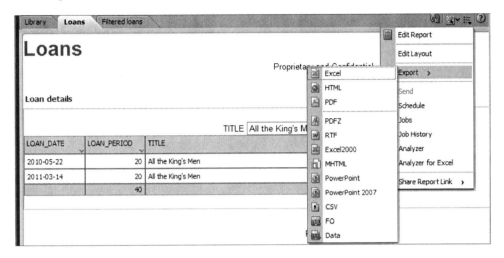

# Summary

After completing this chapter, you should know how to use the Layout Editor Interface, how to add layout elements and set properties for these elements, and how to take advantage of some of the BIP Template features such as automatic filtering and repeating sections.

The Template Builder for MS Word will be the main topic for the next chapter as this is an important tool available for RTF layouts design. It is suitable even when coding is a necessary part of the layout design.

# 6
# Oracle BIP Template Builder for Microsoft Word

Rich Text Format (RTF) layouts are preferred when designing reports that request complex word formatting and processing. The advantage of being designed in Word is that it can use all the formatting tools offered by Microsoft Word.

We saw in *Chapter 4, Report Layout Template* that you can design RTF templates even without the Template Builder. However, this add-in simplifies a lot of your work by enabling the following:

- Insertion of elements such as data fields, tables, or charts
- Template preview with sample XML data
- Translations test

In this chapter, we will go through the most important features of the Template Builder for Word. The 11.1.1.3.0 version of Template Builder for Word along with Microsoft Office Word 2007 was used for these examples. This chapter will cover the following topics:

- BIP and Template Builder interaction
- Insert template elements
- Modify template elements
- Template validation
- Translations

# Installing Template Builder for Word

In order to install the Template Builder, select the **Template Builder for Word** from the options provided for downloading BI Publisher tools on the home page of BIP 11g, as shown in the following screenshot:

Your installation was correct if you can find `TemplateBuilder.dot` in the **Active Application Add-Ins** section of the Word add-ins, which is shown in the following screenshot:

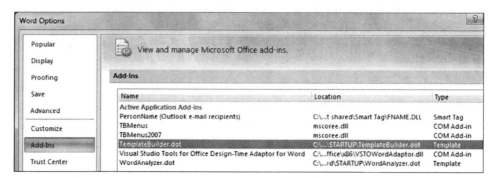

You will get a ribbon type menu in Word 2007, as shown in the following screenshot:

The **BI Publisher** menu—the one which is active—has six groups of tools:

- **Online**
- **Load Data**
- **Insert**
- **Preview**
- **Tools**
- **Options**

We will see how to use these tools into the RTF template building process.

# BIP and Template Builder interaction

For BIP to communicate with the Template Builder and vice versa, multiple ways can be used. They are as follows:

## Upload or generate layout

In order to generate an RTF layout in BIP, use the **Create report interface**, as shown in the following screenshot:

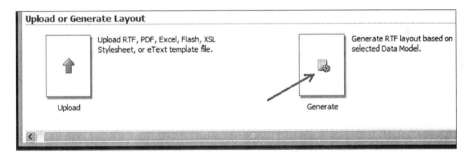

For example, we have a structured Data Layout, which is shown in the following screenshot:

| Data Source | XML View | | | Business View | |
|---|---|---|---|---|---|
| | XML Tag Name | Sorting | Value If Null | Display Name | Data Type |
| ⊟ Report Data | | | | | |
| ⊟ Data Structure | DATA_DS | | | | |
| ⊟ Sales | Sales | | | Sales | |
| 999 INVOICE_ID | INVOICE_ID | ⇕ | | INVOICE_ID | 999 |
| ▦ INVOICE_DATE | INVOICE_DATE | ⇕ | | INVOICE_DATE | ▦ |
| 999 CLIENT_ID | CLIENT_ID | ⇕ | | CLIENT_ID | 999 |
| abc NAME | NAME | ⇕ | | NAME | abc |
| abc ADDRESS | ADDRESS | ⇕ | | ADDRESS | abc |
| abc CITY | CITY | ⇕ | | CITY | abc |
| Σ Products.VALUE | INVOICE_VALUE | ⊘ | | INVOICE_VALUE | 999 |
| ⊟ Sales | Products | | | Products | |
| 999 PRODUCT_ID | PRODUCT_ID | ⊘ | | PRODUCT_ID | 999 |
| abc DESCRIPTION | DESCRIPTION | ⊘ | | DESCRIPTION | abc |
| 999 QUANTITY | QUANTITY | ⊘ | | QUANTITY | 999 |
| abc UM | UM | ⊘ | | UM | abc |
| 999 PRICE | PRICE | ⊘ | | PRICE | 999 |
| ƒx VALUE | VALUE | ⊘ | | VALUE | 999 |

For this structure, BIP generates the following RTF layout:

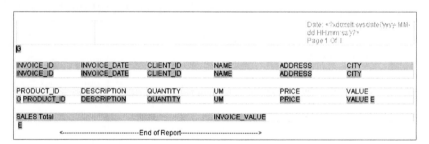

You can see that all the elements of your data source are now displayed in the corresponding form of the RTF layout.

Using the same Create report interface, upload the modified version of the template to BIP that will look similar to the following screenshot:

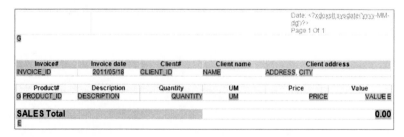

# Login to BIP

Another way of interaction between BIP and the Template Builder for Word is using the **Log On** option of the **BI Publisher** menu that is accessible in Word after installing the Template Builder add-in. After accessing this option, the BIP login interface is displayed as you can see in the following screenshot:

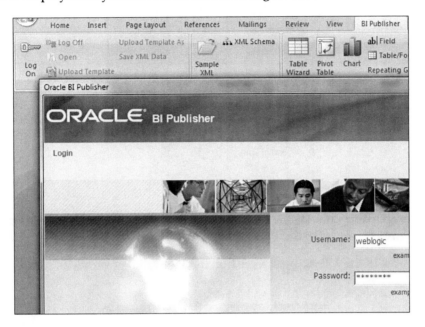

After logging in, you get the following options:

- **Open**: You can open a BIP template
- **Upload Template**: You can upload a Template to BIP
- **Save**: You can save any XML data

# Template preview

Load your previously saved XML data into the Template Builder using the **Sample XML** option, as shown in the following screenshot:

Loading sample data enables the tools for inserting elements, such as fields or charts, into your template and also the **Preview** options.

As you can see in the following screenshot, the **Field** dialog provides sample data for a selected XML field:

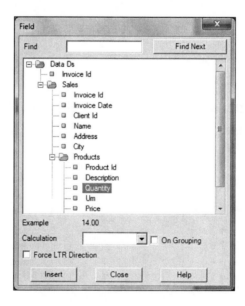

However, for a preview, you can choose from the following formats:

- PDF
- HTML
- Excel
- Excel 2000
- RTF
- PowerPoint

For example, you have the PDF file generated in the following screenshot:

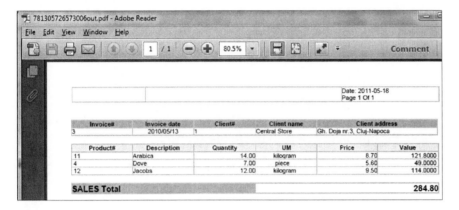

# Insert template elements

In the following sections, you will see how to insert some of the template elements and how to set their properties.

# Text field

In order to get the desired fields into your template, drag-and-drop the fields using the **Field** dialog, as shown in the following screenshot:

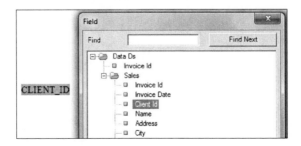

As shown in the following screenshot, double-click on the inserted field and on the **Properties** tab, set the data type and format. On the **Advanced** tab, the code using the BIP syntax, such as `<?CLIENT_ID?>`, is automatically inserted in edit mode:

You also have the option to insert all the fields at once.

For doing so, select the **All Fields** option on the **BI Publisher** menu. For our example, we got the following result:

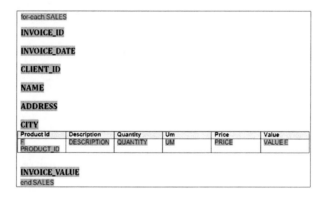

# Chart

Use the **Chart** option from the **BI Publisher** menu to get the **Chart** dialog, which is shown in the following screenshot:

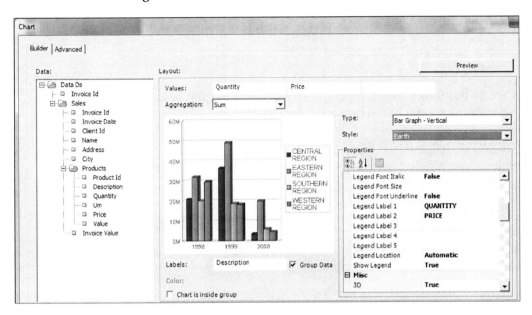

Drag-and-drop the fields **Quantity** and **Price** from the tree view structure of the XML file on the **Values** area and the **Description** field on the **Labels** area. Also choose the **Type** and **Style** for the chart.

The result, using the sample data, is shown in the following screenshot:

 To make changes on your chart, right-click on the chart and go to the **BI Publisher Chart** option of the menu.

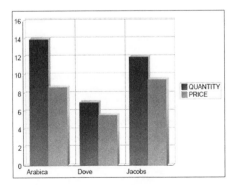

# Conditional region

Use a conditional region to put a filter on your data. Depending on the condition entered, the data matching the criteria only will be shown in the region between the form fields **C** and **EC** that are entered to mark the condition start and end. The underlying code for these fields in our example is as follows:

```
<?if:number(PRODUCT_ID)>10?>
<?end if?>
```

In the **BI Publisher** menu, go to the **Conditional Region** option and enter your condition, as shown in the following screenshot.

Move the **EC** field wherever you want your region to end:

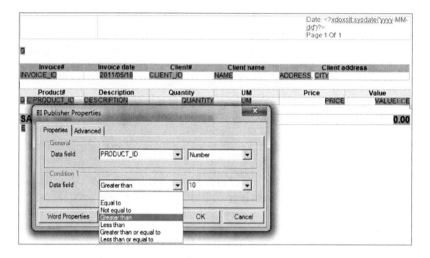

As you can see in the following screenshot, the products were filtered with respect to the entered condition:

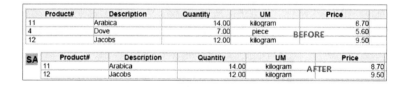

# Table or form

In order to insert a table, go to the **Table/Form** option on the **BI Publisher** menu.

You will get the **Insert Table/Form** interface, which is shown in the following screenshot.

Drag a repeating group marked with bold text in the **Data Source** panel to the **Template** panel. For example, add the **Products** node to the **Template** panel. You are prompted to choose to either drop all the nodes or a single node; however, choose to add a single node. After the parent node is added to the template, you can start with the child nodes:

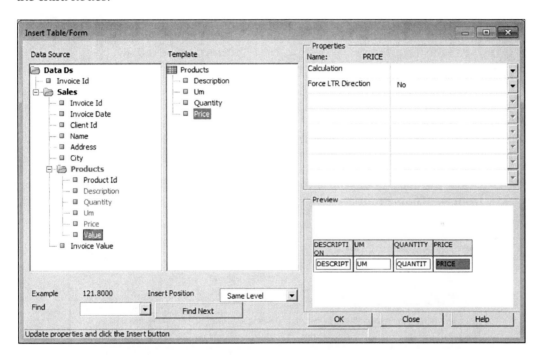

Notice the **Insert Position** option. If you set this option to **Same Level**, you can add nodes to the template by dropping them over nodes having the same level. For example, drag **Value** over **Price**. If the option is set to **Child**, you must drag the child node over its parent. For example, drag **Product Id** over **Products**.

# Modify template elements

A double-click on the template element will display the element's **Properties** dialog. Alternatively, you can right-click on the desired element to get more BI Publisher options in a menu, such as the one shown in the following screenshot:

# Template validation

Multiple options are available when validating your template. In order to check this follow the suggestions given here:

1.  Check the validity of your template by using the **Validate Template** option from the **Tools** group:

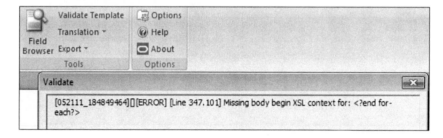

    As you can see in the preceding screenshot, an error message is displayed indicating the error.

    When there are no errors, the text **No Error found** is displayed.

2.  At the same time, a template error makes the preview unavailable and choosing any preview option displays an error window.

3.  In order to check the underlying code of these errors, you have the **Field Browser** option. The **Field Browser** dialog is shown in the following screenshot:

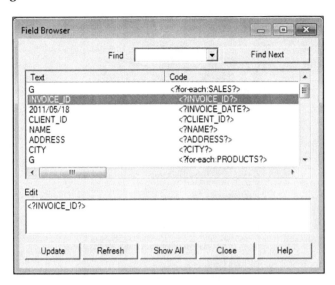

As the preceding screenshot shows, you can search, edit, and update any line that you choose. When a template section is selected, the **Field Browser** displays only the corresponding instructions.

# Translations

When dealing with report translations, consider the following two cases:

*   The translated report has the same layout as the original layout when a XLIFF file has to be used
*   Another layout must be provided for the translation

The following are the steps required for a simple translation, addressing the first case from those we just saw:

1. Go to **Translation | Extract Text** on the BI Publisher tool bar. You will get an XLF file that has a structure similar to the one shown in the following screenshot:

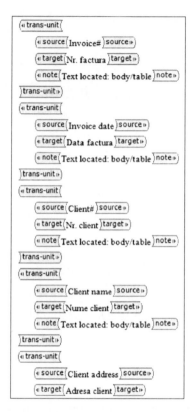

2. Update `<target>` elements with translation of `<source>` elements. For example `Invoice date` from our example template was translated to `Data factura` in Romanian. Also, change the `target-language`, which is an attribute of the `file` element, found at the beginning of the XLF file.

3. Go to **Translation | Preview Translation** and open the previously modified XLF file. You will get the PDF result, as shown in the following screenshot:

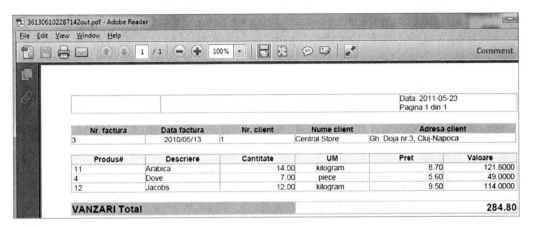

4. Localize your template—this means that you will have the original version of your template replaced by the translated one. For this, you have to go to **Translation | Localize template**.

5. Upload the translated template to BIP.

In the second case, a completely new layout is designed and uploaded to BIP.

Be careful to choose the appropriate locale when uploading a translated template to BIP.

*Appendix A, Report Translations* of the book will offer a more detailed look into report translations.

# Summary

After a detailed look into the Template Builder for Word functionalities, you should be able to communicate between BIP and Template Builder, to insert and modify template elements, to validate your template, and to create a localization for your report.

In the next chapter, we will continue with managing reports, in which we will cover setting report properties, viewing and running reports, consulting job history, and so on.

# The Report Configuration

# 7

Besides Data Model and Layout Template discussed in the previous chapters, BIP deals with some more aspects concerning the report's life. Depending on the properties set for the report, you will get different results. Some BIP features will be enabled or disabled, or your reports will be given different formats. This chapter will also include instructions on managing report jobs and consulting jobs history.

In this chapter, we will cover the following topics:

- Properties settings
- Report Viewer options
- Schedule Report Job
- View report history

# Properties settings

You can set report properties throughout the life cycle of a report starting with its creation.

As you can see in the following screenshot, you have two options available on the home page for starting report creation:

- Click on the **New** drop-down to create a new report.
- Choose the **Report** link from the **Create** section

You will be prompted to choose an existing Data Model for your report. The Create Report interface, shown in the following screenshot, appears as a result of choosing the desired Data Model. The actions available on this interface are quite interesting and essential for report settings. At this point you can:

- Choose or create a Data Model
- Set properties for the report's parameters
- Set report properties
- View a report
- Save a report
- Create or upload a layout

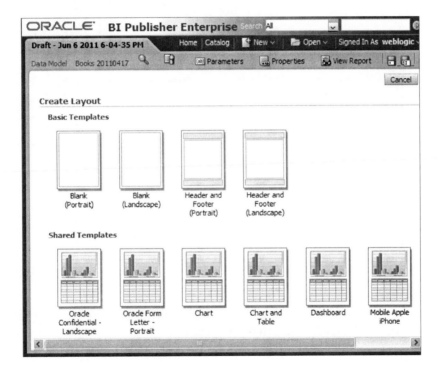

# Parameters

When designing the report's Data Model, the parameters have also been defined (if necessary). Launch the **Parameters** dialog by clicking on **Parameters** in the page header. In this phase, as you can see in the following screenshot, only some display settings can be changed, which are as follows:

- **Show**
- **Display Label**
- **Default Value**
- **Parameters Display per line**

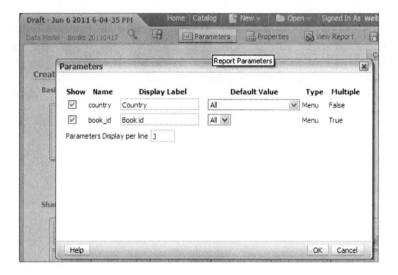

# Properties

Launch the **Report Properties** dialog by clicking on **Properties** in the page header. Report Properties are divided into five categories:

- General
- Caching
- Formatting
- Font Mapping
- Currency Formatting

In the following sections, we will discuss the meaning of these properties and how to set their values in different circumstances.

# General

On the **General** tab, you will find all the properties, as shown in the following screenshot:

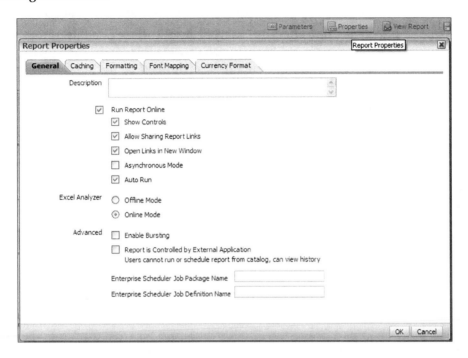

- **Description**: The description is displayed in the Catalog with the report.
- **Run Report Online**: You can disable this option for long-running reports or for reports where online viewing is not appropriate. You can also check the following settings as per your need:
    - **Show controls**: You can disable this option if you don't want the user to control Output, Parameters, and Template lists.
    - **Allow Sharing Report Links**: A URL link is displayed and users can copy the current report link.
    - **Open Links in New Window**: You can open links in a new window using this option.
    - **Asynchronous Mode**: When this option is enabled, the BIP uses a separate execution thread to run the current report. For example, using this option for large reports leads to a BIP increased performance in executing other tasks.
    - **Auto Run**: By disabling this option during report opening, the online viewer will be displayed but without running the report.

- **Excel Analyzer**: It controls the way the BIP interacts with Microsoft Excel.
- **Advanced**: This option provides the following settings:
  - ° **Enable bursting**: If you have a bursting definition in your Data Model, select the definition type to be used for delivering the report.
  - ° **Report is Controlled by External Application**: Use this option in case you don't want users to run or view this report directly from the catalog. These tasks are left to be controlled by the application with which the BIP is integrated.

# Caching

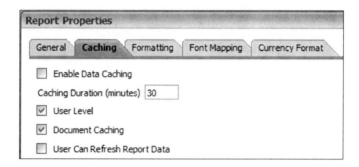

On the **Caching** tab, report properties specifiy how, and for what duration, the data generated by the report will be used. When caching is enabled, a report request having the same parameters will use data stored in the cache. This setting enhances performance by using stored data to generate a report rather than regenerating the data from the source. The data will remain in the cache according to the time limit specified in the **Caching Duration** property. If the **User Can Refresh Report Data** option is enabled, the user can force data refresh. In this case, data stored in the cache will not be used.

# Formatting

This section contains template settings for all the format types that you can use in the BIP.

For example, you can see the Formatting properties settings for a Flash template and settings for a CSV output in the following screenshot:

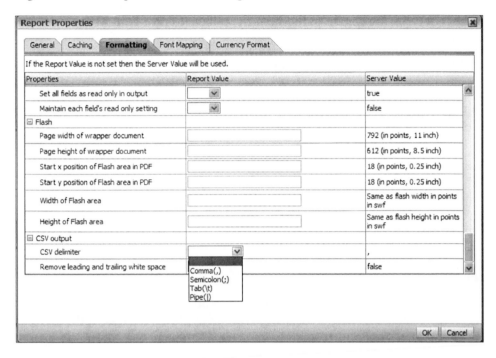

For an RTF Output, you can set the following properties:

- **Enable change tracking**
- **Protect document for tracked changes**
- **Default font**

# Font Mapping

Have you experienced the situation in which everything coming from the BI Publisher looks OK, but in PDF there are question marks like this: **??????? ???????? ????**

This is because other formats use the local machine's fonts but PDF format uses its own fonts.

The solution for this is to add the missing font type
to `$BI_HOME//jdk/jre/lib/fonts/`.

After the font types are copied to the server you have to do a **Font Mapping**
in the BIP:

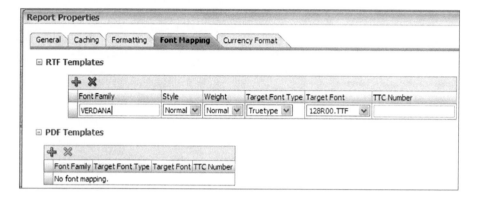

# Currency Format

Set a currency format to have multiple currencies on a single report displayed
in their own format. Currency formatting is only supported for RTF and
XSL-FO templates:

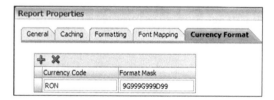

The format mask is in Oracle number format. This is explained by the example
shown in the preceding screenshot:

- 9 (number): Only if present in data
- G: Group separator
- D: Decimal separator
- 0 (explicitly number): May or may not be present in data

# Report Viewer options

Runtime options can be set using the **Report Viewer interface**. One way to access Report Viewer is by opening the report from the home page link, as shown in the following screenshot:

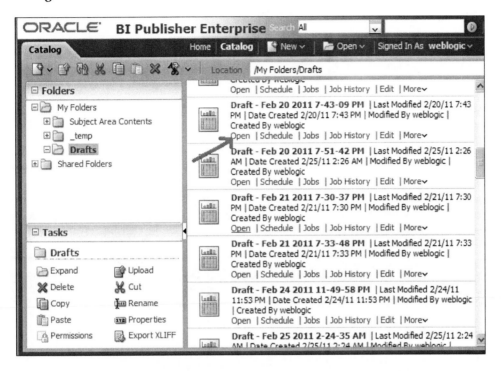

As a result, the Create Report interface is displayed, with the templates attached in the main section as thumbnails or a list.

In the following screenshot, you can see that the **View Thumbnails** option in the upper-right corner is active and you can proceed with the following actions on a template:

- **Add New Layout**
- **Edit**
- **Properties**
- **Delete**

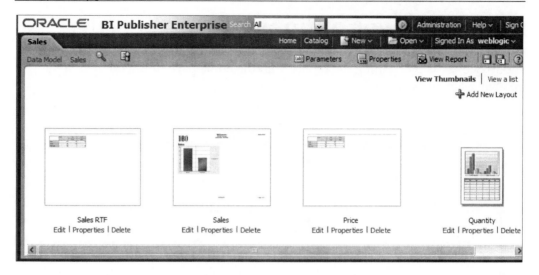

The same actions can be found in the list view of the report templates, as shown in the following screenshot. On the top-left corner of the list, you can see the four icons active for the selected layout:

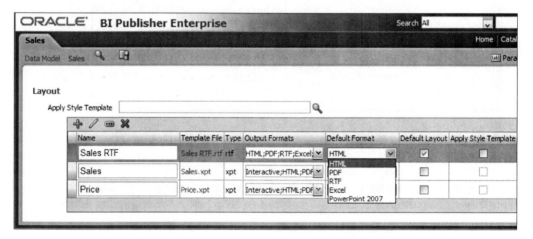

This Properties interface, which is shown in the following screenshot, enables uploading and deleting of templates for different locales and translations. It also manages the extracting, uploading, and deleting of XLIFF files:

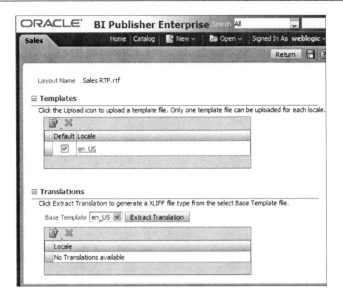

In order to get to the main subject, choose the **View Report** option on the Create Report interface. The **Report viewer** window is displayed as shown in the following screenshot:

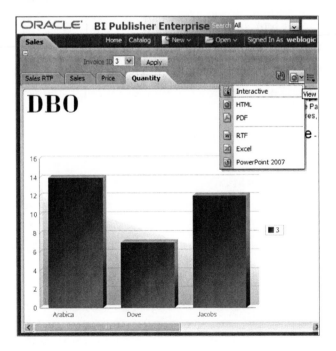

Now, let's go through the components of this interface.

# Parameters

As shown in the preceding screenshot, choose a value for the report's parameter(s) found in the upper section. You have to select **Apply** to have the results displayed on the report according to the new parameter values. For example, choose **3** for **Invoice ID** to get the quantities on that invoice, which is shown in the previous chart.

# Layout

This in the main section of the window. Separate tabs are provided if the report has more than one layout. Here we have four layouts for the **Sales** report:

- **Sales RTF**
- **Sales**
- **Price**
- **Quantity**

# View Report menu

Depending on Properties settings and Template types, the possible values are:

- **Interactive** : For templates designed in the BIP's editor
- **HTML** (Hypertext Markup Language): For any Internet browser
- **PDF** (Portable Document Format): For Adobe Acrobat reader
- **RTF** (Rich Text Format): For word processing applications
- **Excel**: For Microsoft Excel 2003 or later
- **Excel 2000**: For Microsoft Excel 2000 or 2002
- **PowerPoint**: For Microsoft PowerPoint 2003
- **PowerPoint 2007**: For Microsoft PowerPoint 2007
- **Flash**: Flash templates will open in a browser that needs Adobe flash Player plugin installed
- **CSV** (Comma Separated Values): For a file containing data stored in plain-text delimited by a symbol
- **Data**: It will display data in XML format

- **MHTML** (Mime Hypertext Markup Language): Saves an HTML page as a single `.mht` file
- **PDFZ** (Zipped PDF): Split PDF saved in a `.zip` file along with an index file
- **FO**: The result is an XML file with XLS-FO information

# Actions menu

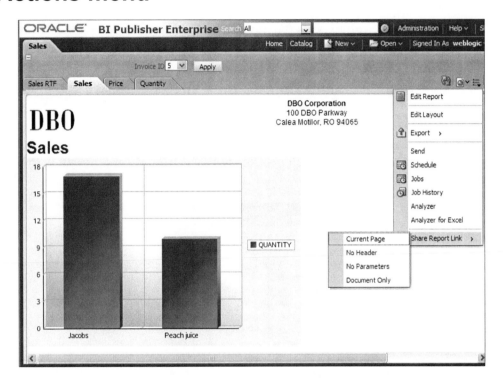

This menu contains options depending on user privileges and report properties settings, and the complete list of these options is as follows:

- **Edit Report**: Opens the Create Report interface.
- **Edit Layout**: Enables you to open or create layouts.
- **Export** : Exports the report to the default application for the selected output type.

- **Send**: Enables report scheduling for delivery by launching Schedule Report Job (will be discussed later in this chapter).

- **Schedule**: Creates a report job (will be discussed later in this chapter).

- **Jobs**: Opens the currently scheduled jobs manager for this report.

- **Job History**: Offers a view of completed report jobs.

- **Analyzer**: Launches the Online Analyzer, which enables you to create a pivot table using current data.

- **Analyzer for Excel**: Exports the report data to Microsoft Excel.

- **Share Report Link**: You can copy and reuse the report link. As you can see, different options regarding the page content are available.

# Schedule Report Job

There are many ways to get to the report jobs scheduler interface. As you can see in the following screenshot, one such possible option is **Report Job**, present in the **Create** section of the home page:

Some other available options are:

- Access **Catalog**, find the report you want to schedule, and click on the **Schedule** link

- From the **Report Viewer** go to **Actions** and then to **Schedule**

The **Schedule Report Job** page contains four tabs to define the options for your report job: **General**, **Output**, **Schedule**, and **Notification**.

# General

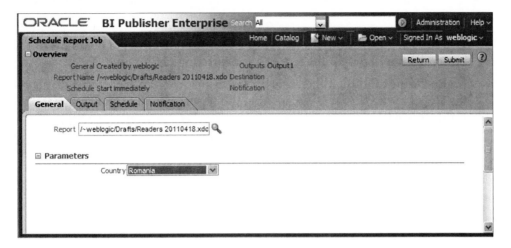

The **General** tab, shown in the preceding screenshot, contains the report name if you accessed the Schedule page from the report, or allows you to browse for the desired report.

On this tab, you have to also choose the values for the report parameters. The selected values will be used for the current schedule.

# Output

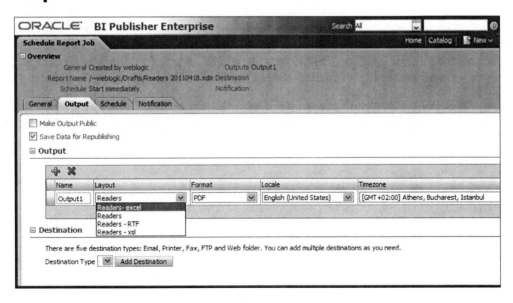

As you can see in the preceding screenshot, on the **Output** tab you can set the output properties and add destinations for the report. First, you have some options that concern all the outputs:

- **Use Bursting Definition to determine Output & Delivery Destination**: This option is shown only if the report has a bursting definition
- **Make Output Public**: When this option is enabled, the report will display in the **Report Job History** page, making the report available to all users with rights to see it
- **Save Data for Republishing**: XML data generated for this job will be saved

Then, for each new output, you have to enter or set the following properties:

- **Name**
- **Layout**
- **Format**
- **Locale**
- **Timezone**
- **Calendar**
- **Save Output**

Also, set the delivery options in the **Destination** area. In order to add destinations, you need to set up Delivery servers in the Administration interface but this job is usually done by the BIP's administrator.

# Schedule

A recurrence pattern is defined in the **Schedule** tab. As you can see in the following screenshot, four dimensions are available in the **Define Schedule Time** section:

- **Frequency**: You can choose one of the following values for this parameter:
  - Once
  - Hourly/Minute
  - Daily
  - Weekly
  - Monthly
  - Annually
  - Specific Dates

- **Every**: Enter an integer value as the increment value
- **Start**: Choose the date and time to start running the schedule
- **End**: Choose the date and time to stop running the schedule

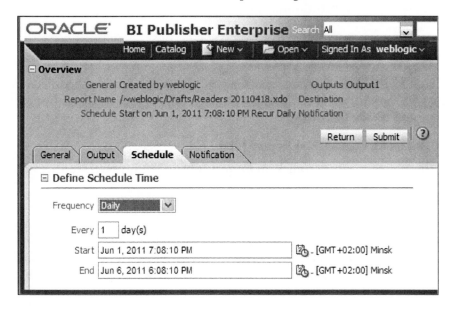

Depending on the chosen frequency, a slight modification can occur in these parameters. For example, when the **Monthly** frequency is chosen, the **On** parameter is added to specify a day of the week or a specific date in the month.

# Notification

Add notifications if you want to inform a user via e-mail or HTTP of a report status. Possible statuses that can be set for a report are:

- Completed
- Completed with warnings
- Failed

To use this feature, the BI Publisher administrator configures e-mail, FTP, or HTTP servers using the **Delivery** section of the Administration interface.

# Submit the job

In order to submit the job, click on the **Submit** button (shown in the preceding screenshot). The **Submit Job** dialog will be displayed. Review the details, enter a name for the job, and click **Submit**.

# Manage report jobs

The **Manage Report Jobs** interface enables you to manage future scheduled and recurring jobs for your reports. Go to the Manage Report Jobs interface from the home page and do the following:

- Click on **Open** and then **Report Jobs**
- Alternatively, you can click on **Report Jobs** in the **Browse/Manage** area

The available actions on a report job are delete, pause, and resume. We will see, which are the usual steps when performing such a task.

First, click on the **Select time zone to view jobs** drop-down and then click on **Refresh**. This will display the appropriate values for **Start Time** and **End Time** by using the selected time zone, as shown in the following screenshot, which shows the Manage Report Jobs interface:

Next, enter **filters** to quicken the process of finding the jobs you need. As you can see in the preceding screenshot, in the **Filters** region, the following default filters are present:

- **Owner**: Checks with your user ID.

- **Scope**: Select the required scope from the drop-down. **All** implies that all the public and private jobs will be included.
- **Status** : Select the required scope from the drop-down. **All** implies that both active and suspended jobs will be included.

Enter more filtering criteria (besides combinations of those already mentioned) using the following filters:

- **Report Job Name**
- **Report Name**
- **Start Time**
- **End Time**

Click on the **Report Job** name to view a **detail** page for the job.

Select one or more jobs by clicking on the table rows and then click on the icons in the left corner of the jobs table to **delete** or **pause** a report job.

In order to resume a suspended job, choose the job and then click on the corresponding icon.

# View report history

The **Report Job History** interface displays information about running and completed report jobs. In order to go to the Report Job History interface from the home page:

- Click **Open** and then **Report Job History**
- Alternatively, click on **Report Job History** in the **Browse/Manage** area

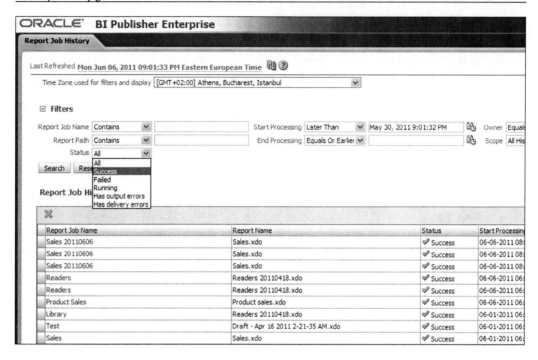

As you can see in the preceding screenshot, which shows the Report Job History interface, default values were used for some parameters to display the current list:

- **Start Processing**: Equals to or later than: **May 30** (usually a date which is one week earlier than the current date is displayed automatically).

- **Owner**: Checks with your user ID.

- **Scope**: Select the required scope from the drop-down. **All** implies that all the histories will be displayed including public and private job histories.

- **Status**: Select the required scope from the drop-down. **All** implies that all the statuses will be displayed (success, failed, running, has output errors, and has delivery errors statuses are included)

Click the **Report Job Name** to view a **detail** page for the job. Besides consulting report job details, you can use this page to:

- Download XML data
- Republish the report
- Send the output to a new destination

# Report Job's life

Schedule Report Job, Manage Report Jobs, and Report Job History interfaces can also be accessed from the context of a specific report. As you can see in the following screenshot, go to the report in Catalog and you have **Schedule**, **Jobs**, and **Job History** links under the report name. The same functionalities for a report are implemented as actions in the **Actions** menu of the Report Viewer interface.

As a recap, let's follow a report job from the time it is submitted until its complete history can be viewed:

1. Open the **Catalog** tab on the home page.
2. Navigate to a report.
3. Click on **Schedule** — the link under the report's name, as shown in the following screenshot:

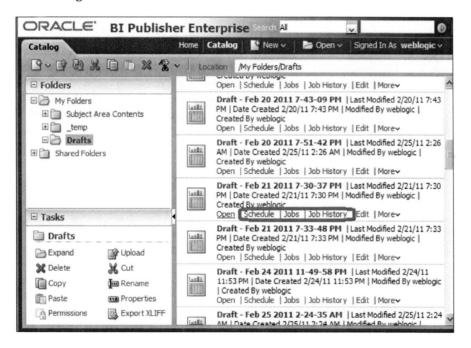

4. On the Schedule Report Job interface, select **Parameters**, and set **Output**, **Schedule**, and **Notification** properties, as shown in the following screenshot:

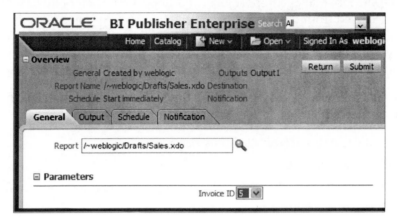

5. Click on **Submit**.

6. This will display the **Submit Job** dialog with information for you to review. Enter **Report Job Name** and click **Submit**, as shown in the following screenshot:

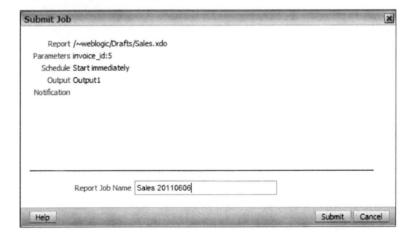

7. Click on the **Jobs** link under the report's name in the **Catalog** tab. As you can see in the following screenshot, **Report Name** was already used as a criteria to filter the report jobs:

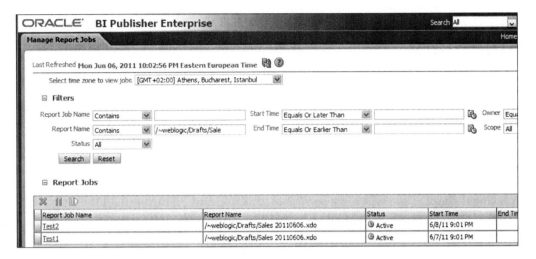

8. Click on the actions of a selected report job's corresponding icons to delete, pause, or resume the performance.

9. Click on the **Report Job history** link under the report's name. You will get the Report Job History interface as shown in the following screenshot:

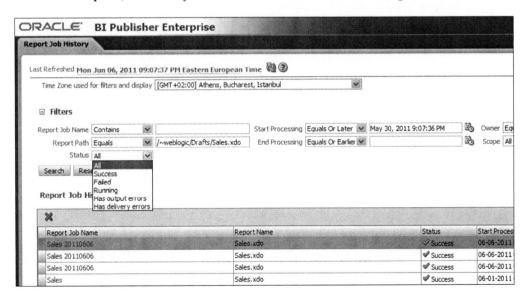

10. Delete report job from history by clicking on the corresponding icon.

11. View the **detail** page and download the XML data produced by the report job.

# Summary

We can consider a report designed using the BIP as a complex entity; the benefits of using BIP are the numerous properties and tools offered to suit the user's needs better and to facilitate the designer's approach in following a report's status in every stage of its life. This chapter proposes a practical guide for setting report properties, setting viewing options, and taking actions on a report. After completing this chapter, you should also know how to deal with report jobs as this is an important step in a report's life.

In the next chapter, we will see a complete example and go through all the stages of a report's life from creating the Data Model to consulting the Job History.

# 8

# Exploring BI Publisher 11g: A Simple Report Example

We've been busy in the earlier chapters analyzing the report's structure in BIP, taking a more in-depth look at its components, behavior, and tools used to create its data sources structure, to design its layout, to translate, to set its properties, and finally, to manage report jobs. To get a comprehensive view of all these mechanisms, this chapter will show a complete example for you to follow when designing a report, considering the following points:

- Data Model
- Layout Template
- Report configuration
- Report Job
- Translation

## Data Model

First, create the data source's structure using the **Data Model Editor** interface. Although there is more than one way to get to the same point, we'll choose a precise path for our example. So, we will use the following steps to create your Data Model:

1. On the BIP homepage, select **Data Model** from the **Create** section. The **Data Model Editor** interface will be displayed.

2. Set the Data Model properties.

3. In the left menu, go to **Data Sets**.

4. On the toolbar, select **SQL Query** to create a SQL Query type data set.

5. Enter a **Name**, choose the **Data Source**, and open the **Query Builder interface**.

6. Choose your tables, create links between them, and check all the fields you want to display on your report. For this example, you have the structure displayed in the following screenshot:

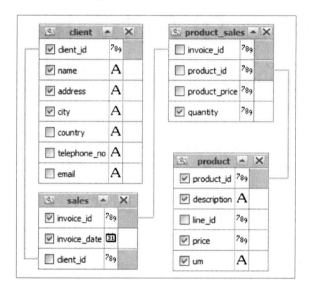

7. In the **Query Builder interface**, go to the **Results** window to take a look at your data. You'll find in this view, data from all selected columns.

8. **Save** your query:

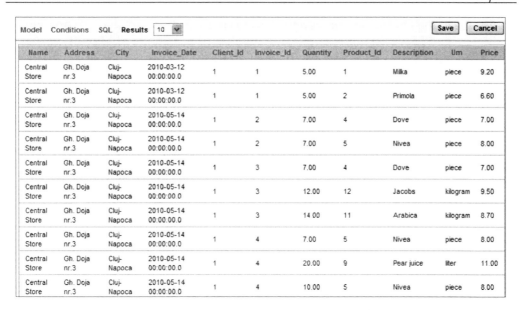

| Name | Address | City | Invoice_Date | Client_Id | Invoice_Id | Quantity | Product_Id | Description | Um | Price |
|---|---|---|---|---|---|---|---|---|---|---|
| Central Store | Gh. Doja nr.3 | Cluj-Napoca | 2010-03-12 00:00:00.0 | 1 | 1 | 5.00 | 1 | Milka | piece | 9.20 |
| Central Store | Gh. Doja nr.3 | Cluj-Napoca | 2010-03-12 00:00:00.0 | 1 | 1 | 5.00 | 2 | Primola | piece | 6.60 |
| Central Store | Gh. Doja nr.3 | Cluj-Napoca | 2010-05-14 00:00:00.0 | 1 | 2 | 7.00 | 4 | Dove | piece | 7.00 |
| Central Store | Gh. Doja nr.3 | Cluj-Napoca | 2010-05-14 00:00:00.0 | 1 | 2 | 7.00 | 5 | Nivea | piece | 8.00 |
| Central Store | Gh. Doja nr.3 | Cluj-Napoca | 2010-05-14 00:00:00.0 | 1 | 3 | 7.00 | 4 | Dove | piece | 7.00 |
| Central Store | Gh. Doja nr.3 | Cluj-Napoca | 2010-05-14 00:00:00.0 | 1 | 3 | 12.00 | 12 | Jacobs | kilogram | 9.50 |
| Central Store | Gh. Doja nr.3 | Cluj-Napoca | 2010-05-14 00:00:00.0 | 1 | 3 | 14.00 | 11 | Arabica | kilogram | 8.70 |
| Central Store | Gh. Doja nr.3 | Cluj-Napoca | 2010-05-14 00:00:00.0 | 1 | 4 | 7.00 | 5 | Nivea | piece | 8.00 |
| Central Store | Gh. Doja nr.3 | Cluj-Napoca | 2010-05-14 00:00:00.0 | 1 | 4 | 20.00 | 9 | Pear juice | liter | 11.00 |
| Central Store | Gh. Doja nr.3 | Cluj-Napoca | 2010-05-14 00:00:00.0 | 1 | 4 | 10.00 | 5 | Nivea | piece | 8.00 |

9. Go to **List of Values** in the menu on the left in the **Data Model Editor** interface and create **List of Values (LOV)**. The **invoice_id** LOV was created for this example as shown in the following screenshot:

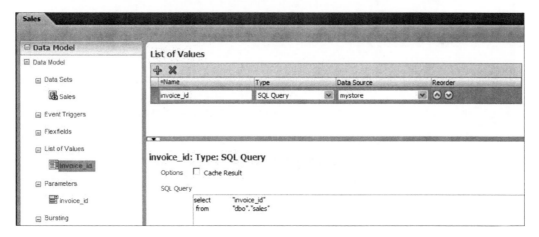

10. Go to the **Parameters** link on the left, to create parameters that use previously created LOVs. In this example, the **invoice_id** parameter of **Menu** type was added. On this page you also have to set the Menu properties as shown in the following screenshot:

    ◦ Display Label
    ◦ List of Values
    ◦ Options

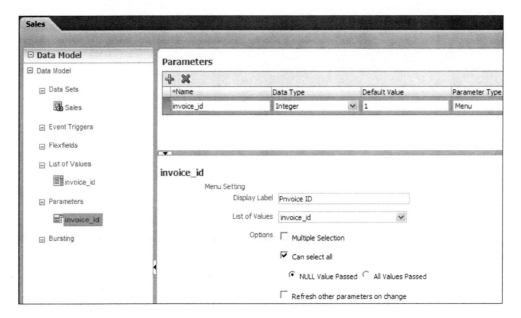

11. Click on the newly created data set in the **Diagram** view and access the data set menu:

12. Group the header data using **Group by** and **Move selected elements to Parent Group** options from the menu as shown in the following screenshot. As a result of these actions, we'll have the **Sales** as the parent group and **Sales_1** as the child group:

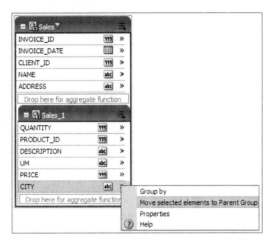

13. Right-click on the group and choose **Add Element by Expressions** to create new calculated elements. For example, the column **VALUE** was added as the result of **QUANTITY * PRICE** as this column's Properties window shows in the following screenshot. Valid combinations of data on the left (data columns or parameters) and operators on the bottom are allowed. Don't forget to have your data validated—click on **Validate Expression**.

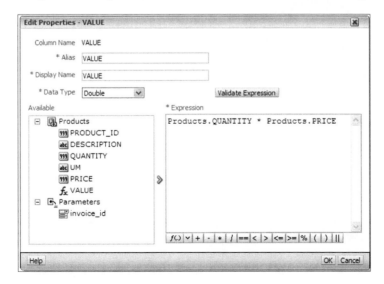

14. Click on OK to go back to the **Data Model Editor** interface.

15. Create aggregate elements by dragging values from the child group (**Sales_1** is our child group) and dropping them into the area marked for aggregated function of the parent group (**Sales** is our parent group). In this example, we'll get **INVOICE_VALUE** column by summing the **VALUE** column:

16. Enter group filters using the created parameters. In order to do this, go to the group menu and click on the **Create Group Filter** option. A filter on the **INVOICE_ID** column was created by entering the expression depending on the **invoice_id** parameter as you can see in the following screenshot:

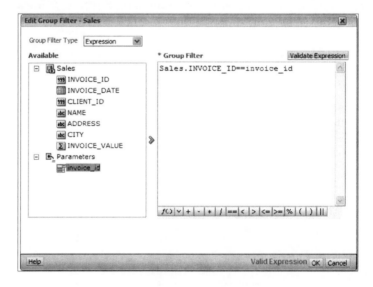

17. Use the Data Model's **Structure** to set:
    ° XML Tag Name
    ° Value if Null
    ° Display Name

Changing value on this tab is optional, but it brings, in certain cases, a visible improvement to the final look of your report, as follows:

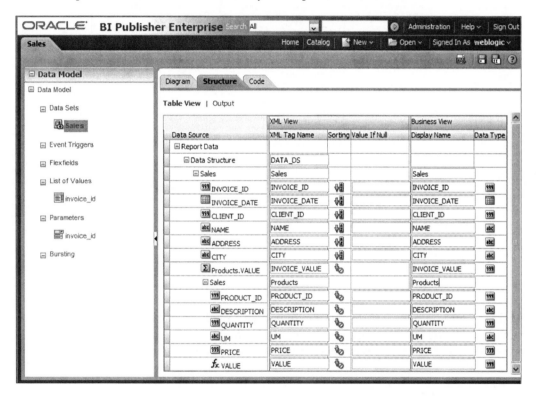

18. It will be very useful to have a sample of your data attached to the Data Model when designing the report's layout (you cannot test the report's layout design without an XML sample). Go through the following steps to save a sample of your data:

    ° Go to **Get XML output** in the icons menu.
    ° On the page displaying the XML output, choose values for your parameters. In this case, for the **Invoice ID** parameter.

- ° Choose a value for the **Number of rows to return** variable.
- ° Click on Run.
- ° Go to the **Actions** menu and choose the **Save As Sample Data** option:

At this point you have a Data Model created and ready to use for your report. For more info on the Data Model see *Chapter 2, Creating a Data Model for a Report* of this book. So you can proceed with the report's layout design.

# Layout Template

To create a Layout Template for your report, perform the following steps:

1. On the BIP homepage select **Report** from the **Create** section.
2. Choose the Data Model you've created when prompted to **Choose Existing Data Model**. Click on **Open**.

3. On the **Create report interface**, choose the type of template to create or upload. You can also choose to generate an RTF template. For this example let's choose to create a **Chart** type template from the **Shared Templates** group:

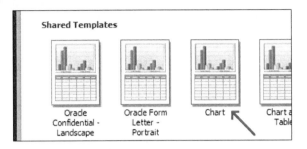

4. Insert report template elements by dragging and dropping them from the left menu **Components** or from the **Insert** tab of the toolbar to the main area of the **Layout Editor interface**. By choosing the **Chart** type template we already have a chart element inserted:

5. Drag data fields to the marked areas. You can see that for a chart there are two marked areas: **Drop Value Here** and **Drop Label Here**:

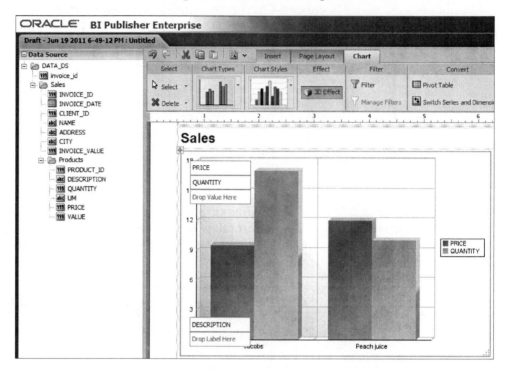

- ◦ Insert **PRICE** and **QUANTITY** fields as values in the chart.
- ◦ Insert **DESCRIPTION** as the label.

6. Set the chart properties using the **Properties** menu on the left, or the **Chart** tab on the **Layout Editor**'s toolbar. As you can see in the following screenshot, to set the color for the chart label font go to **Properties | Chart Label | Font Color** and pick a color:

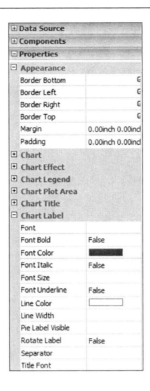

7. Save the layout. On the **Save Layout** dialog, enter the **Layout Name** and don't forget to choose the **Locale**, as locale information is used when matching a layout with the user's account preferences. For more information on this read *Appendix A, Report Translations* of this book:

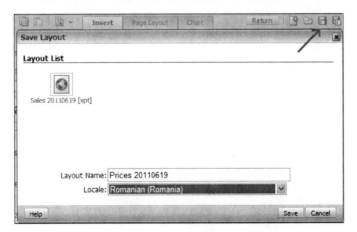

8. Click on **Return** to close the Layout Editor and return to the **Create Report interface**.

9. On the **Create Report interface**, save the report as shown in the following screenshot:

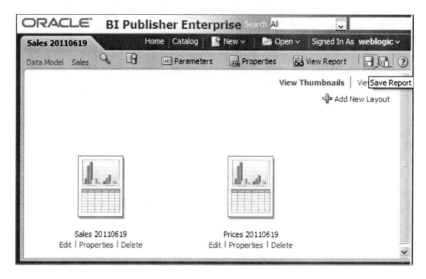

10. Go to the **Report Viewer interface** by clicking on the **View Report** option.

11. Choose a value for the **Invoice ID** parameter. Click on **Apply**.

12. Export the report as a PDF file: Go to the **Actions** menu and choose **Export | PDF**:

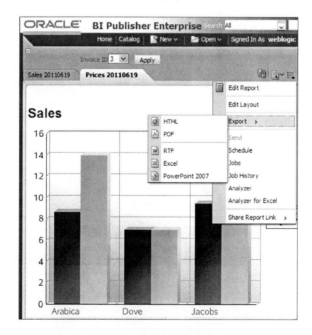

Following the preceding steps, you have completed the first version of your report and its PDF format was successfully generated. For this we used the report's default settings and the report was instantly generated. Also, we didn't provide any translation. We'll deal with these details (important details), in the following part of this chapter.

# Report configuration

Configuring a report consists mainly of setting properties for the report and for the report's parameters. To configure your report perform the following steps:

1. In the **Create Report interface**, select the **Properties** option to open the **Report Properties dialog**. Set the main properties on the **General** tab as shown in the following screenshot:

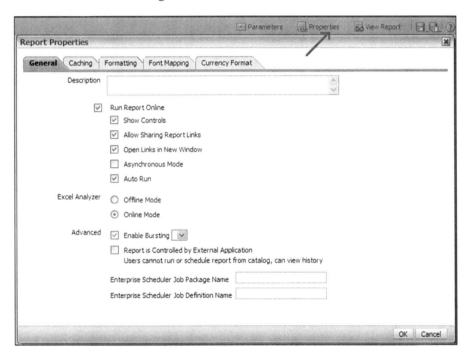

2.  Set formatting properties on the **Formatting** tab. For example, set a password for access to the open PDF outputs. Click on **OK**:

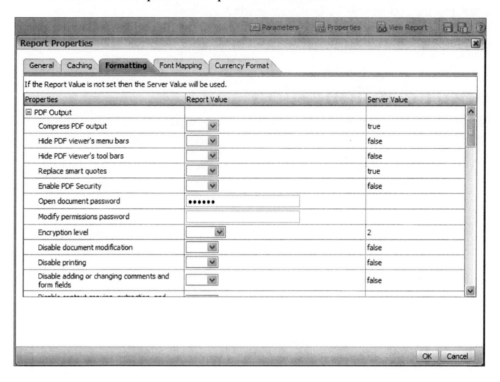

3.  Choose **Parameters** on the **Create Report interface** to set properties for the report's parameters, in the **Parameters dialog** window. For the **invoice_id** parameter set the following values, as shown in the following screenshot:

    ◦  **Show** - This checkbox should be checked
    ◦  **Display Label** - Set the Display Lable as **Invoice ID**
    ◦  **Default Value** - Set this value as **2**

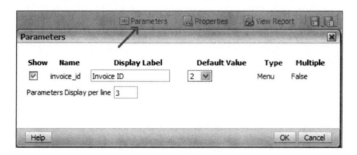

# Report job

Concerning report jobs, the actions you can take are: submit report jobs, manage report jobs, and consult the history list of report jobs. The following steps will take you through the details of these actions:

1. To schedule a report job go to the **Schedule** option in the **Actions** menu in the **Report Viewer interface**:

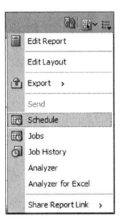

2. The **Schedule Report Job** interface is displayed. On the **General** tab you can see that the report's name (including the path) is already provided and you have to choose the parameter's values that will be used when running this job:

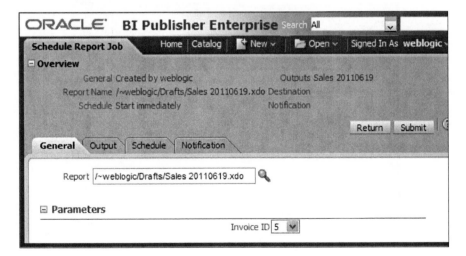

3.  Go to the **Output** tab to enter the output name and to choose either of the following options:

    ° Layout
    ° Format
    ° Locale
    ° Timezone
    ° Calendar
    ° Save output

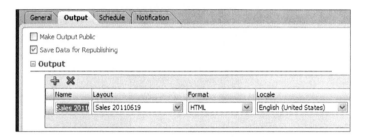

4.  Set time-related parameters in the **Define Schedule Time** section. As you can guess from the following screenshot, there are endless possible combinations available to define your report's schedule.

    Our report will run every hour starting from June 19 at 10:34 P.M. to June 24 at 9:34 P.M:

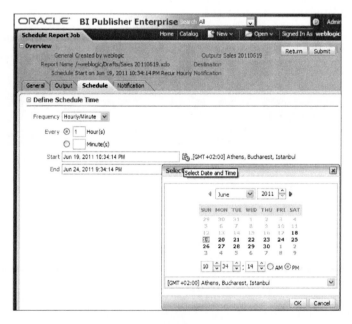

5. Click on **Submit**. This will display the **Submit Job dialog** for you to check on the final settings. Enter **Report Job Name** and submit the job:

6. Navigate to **Open | Report Jobs** to monitor your current report job:

This will display the **Manage Report Jobs interface**.

7. Enter one or more filter fields, like the one from the following screenshot, and click on **Search** to get your report listed in the **Report Jobs** area. The actions you may take on the report job are as follows:

    ° Delete

    ° Pause

    ° Resume

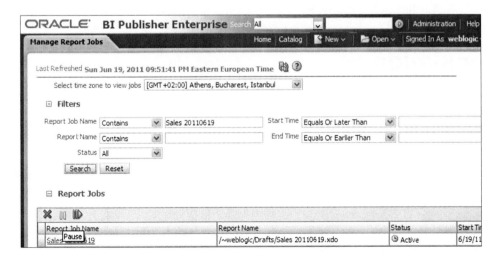

8.  Navigate to **Open | Report Job History** to check the status of your running and completed report jobs:

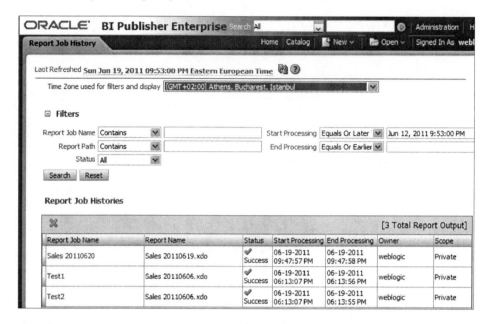

As you can see in the preceding screenshot, our report job ended successfully. Other possible values for a report job status are as follows:

- failed
- running
- has output errors
- has delivery errors

# Translation

We have one more task to be done in order to complete our report's odyssey: the translation.

1.  On the **Report Viewer interface** go to the **Actions** menu and choose **Export | RTF:**

2. In MS Word go to **Translation | Extract Text...** on the BI Publisher tool bar:

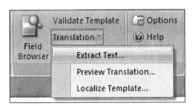

3. In the XLIFF file, update the `<target>` elements with the translation of the `<source>` elements:

```
<trans-unit id="67c2b8f7" maxbytes="4000" maxwidth="37" size-
  unit="char" translate="yes">
  <source>Page [&amp;1]of [&amp;2]</source>
  <target>Pagina [&amp;1]din [&amp;2]</target>
  <prop-group name="ora_reconstruction">
    <prop prop-type="e1">PGZvOnBhZ2UtbnVtYmVyLz4=</prop>
      <prop prop-type="e2">
        PGZvOnBhZ2UtbnVtYmVyLWNpdGF0aW9uIHJl
        Zi1pZD0ieGRvZm86bGFzdHBhZ2Utam9pbnNlSIvPg==</prop>
          </prop-group>
          <note>Text located: footer/table, token &amp;1
,&amp;2:anonymous placeholder(s)</note>
        </trans-unit>
        <trans-unit id="4bf58ec" maxbytes="4000" maxwidth="23"
size-unit="char" translate="yes">
          <source>Sales</source>
          <target>Vanzari</target>
          <note>Text located: body/table</note>
      </trans-unit>
```

4. Go to **Translation | Localize Template...** on the BI Publisher toolbar and open your modified XLF file when prompted.

5. Upload your localized template to BIP.

# Summary

This example was meant to draw the "red line" of report designing in BIP from its Data Model to translation. As a result of following the steps described in this chapter, now you should be dealing with easier report components and knowing BIP's interfaces and their purposes much better.

In the next chapter we'll go on to discussing BIP and e-Business Suite integration.

# 9
# BI Publisher 11g and E-Business Suite

Along with the new 11.1.1.5 release of BIP came the integration with **E-Business Suite (EBS)** capability. You can use EBS's security to navigate to BI Publisher and also to return to the EBS within a context from BIP. As the functionalities require a lot of system configuration, this chapter will provide only a brief introduction of the subject. This chapter will cover:

- Setting up Oracle BI to use Oracle EBS security to authenticate users
- Using actions to integrate Oracle BI with Oracle EBS

## Set up Oracle BI to use Oracle EBS security to authenticate users

Taking EBS as the beginning point, there are a few steps to complete in order to enable the communication with Oracle BI (BIP in particular).

## Integrate EBS database into the Oracle BI repository

To enable integration with Oracle EBS, you must create a **database object** and **connection pool** for the EBS database in the Oracle BI repository.

To create a database object go to the Oracle BI Administration page found in:

**Programs | Oracle Business Intelligence | BI Administration**

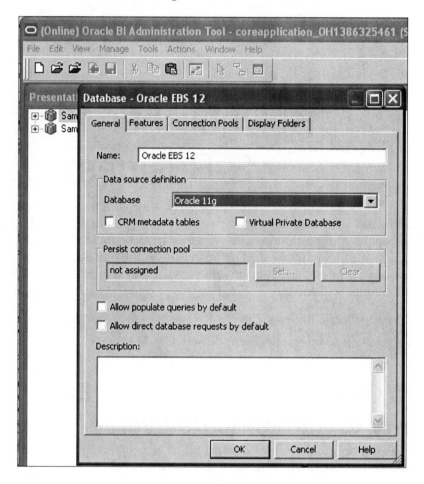

Open the repository that you want to integrate with Oracle EBS. Right-click on the physical layer and select **New Database**. Enter a name and select the database type:

1.  **Name**: Enter a name for the new database (for example, Oracle EBS 12).

2.  **Database**: Select the appropriate Oracle Database type for your Oracle EBS database (for example, Oracle 10g R2 or Oracle 11g).

3.  Click on **OK**.

In order to create a connection pool, right-click on the created database object and go
to **New Object | Connection Pool**:

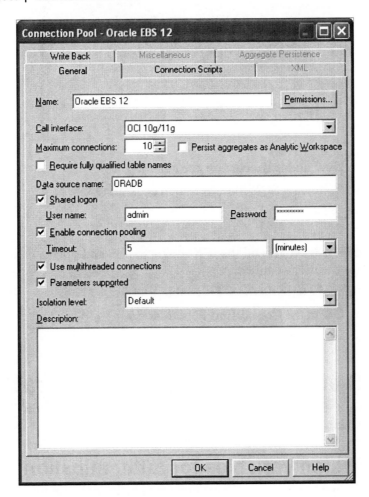

Then, carry out the following steps:

1. Enter a name for the connection pool (for example, Oracle *EBS* 12).

2. In the **Call interface** field select OCI 10g/11g.

3. In the **Data source name** field enter the TNS name of the Oracle
   EBS database.

4. In the **Username** and **Password** fields enter the username and password of
   the Oracle EBS super user.

   Use a super user to ensure access to all administrative functions in case of
   failures with the configured security model.

5. Select the **Connection Scripts** tab:

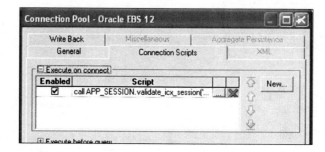

6. Click on **New** under **Execute on connect**.

7. Enter the following SQL code, and then click on **OK**:

```
call APP_SESSION.validate_icx_session
  ('valueof(NQ_SESSION.ICX_SESSION_COOKIE)')
```

This script is used to send the ICX cookie to EBS and open a database session based on the user's context.

8. Check to make sure this script is enabled.

9. Click on **OK** in the **Connection Pool** dialog.

10. Save the repository.

# Use EBS authentication to access Oracle BI

To enable EBS authentication when accessing Oracle BI, set up session variables and update the `authenticationschemas.xml` and `instanceconfig.xml` files.

## Set up session variables for authentication

In the Oracle BI repository, the configuration steps include the set up of eight session variables and an initialization block.

**To set up session variables for authentication in the Administration Tool**, open the repository that you want to integrate with Oracle E-Business Suite and carry out the following steps:

1. Navigate to **Manage | Variables**. The **Variable Manager** dialog box will be displayed.

2. Go to the **Action** menu and select **New | Session | Initialization Block**:

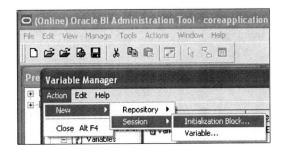

3. Enter a name for the initialization block (for example, Oracle E-Business SSO).

4. Click on **Edit Data Source**, as shown in the following screenshot:

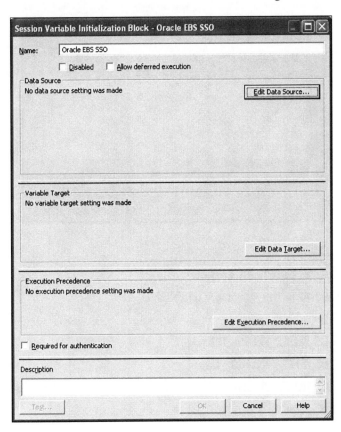

5. For **Default initialization string,** enter the following SQL code:

```
SELECT
   FND_GLOBAL.RESP_ID,
   FND_GLOBAL.RESP_APPL_ID,
   FND_GLOBAL.SECURITY_GROUP_ID,
   FND_GLOBAL.RESP_NAME,
   FND_GLOBAL.USER_ID,
   FND_GLOBAL.EMPLOYEE_ID,
   FND_GLOBAL.USER_NAME
FROM DUAL
```

6. For **Connection Pool**. Click on **Browse**, select the connection pool you created for the Oracle EBS database (for example, Oracle EBS 12), and click on **Select**, as shown in the following screenshot:

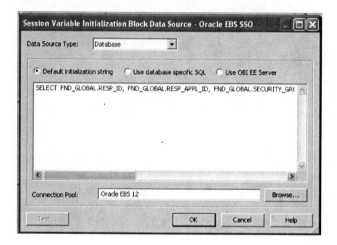

7. Click on **OK**.
8. Then, click on **Edit Data Target**.
9. Create the following session variables:
   ° EBS_RESP_ID
   ° EBS_RESP_APPL_ID
   ° EBS_SEC_GROUP_ID
   ° EBS_RESP_NAME
   ° EBS_USER_ID
   ° EBS_EMPLOYEE_ID
   ° USER

10. To do this, click on **New**, enter the variable name, and then click on **OK**. Click on **Yes** when you receive a warning about the special purpose of the USER variable.

11. Click on **OK** in the Session Variable Initialization Block Variable Target dialog.

12. In the Session Variable Initialization Block dialog, select **Required for authentication**.

13. Click on **OK**.

14. Save the repository.

# Update authenticationschemas.xml

Update the `authenticationschemas.xml` file to add the name of the EBS ICX authentication cookie. In order to do this, open the file in edit mode. The file `authenticationschemas.xml` can be found at:

```
ORACLE_HOME/bifoundation/web/display
```

Then perform the following steps:

1. Find the following element:
   ```
   <AuthenticationSchema name="EBS-ICX"
   ```

2. Locate the sub-element `RequestVariable source="cookie"` and change the value of the `nameInSource` attribute from `ICX_SESSION` to the name of the EBS ICX authentication cookie prefix. For example:
   ```
   <RequestVariable source="cookie" type="auth" nameInSource="VIS"
     biVariableName="NQ_SESSION.ICX_SESSION_COOKIE" />
   ```

3. Do not update the `RequestVariable source="url"` sub-element.

4. In the same entry (`RequestVariable source="cookie"`), ensure that the value of the `biVariableName` attribute is the same as the value you entered as part of the connection script when you created the connection pool for the Oracle EBS database.

5. Find the following element:
   ```
   <SchemaKeyVariable source="cookie"
   ```

6. Change the value of the `nameInSource` attribute from `ICX_SESSION` to the name of the EBS ICX authentication cookie prefix (often `VIS`). For example:
   ```
   <SchemaKeyVariable source="cookie" nameInSource="VIS"
     forceValue="EBS-ICX"/>
   ```

7. Save the file and close it.

# Update instanceconfig.xml

The instanceconfig.xml file will be updated to add EBS-ICS as one of the enabled schemas, and set it as the default. In order to do this, open it in Edit mode. The instanceconfig.xml file can be found at:

```
ORACLE_INSTANCE/config/OracleBIPresentationServicesComponent/
coreapplication_obipsn
```

Then follow these steps:

1. Locate the Authentication element.
2. Include EBS-ICX in the list of enabled schemas. For example:

   ```
   <EnabledSchemas>UidPwd,Impersonate,UidPwd-soap,Impersonate-soap,
      EBS-ICX</EnabledSchemas>
   ```

3. Ignore the comment in instanceconfig.xml that says this setting is centrally managed. EBS-ICX must be manually added to the EnabledSchemas element.
4. Save the file and close it.
5. Restart Oracle BI.

# Include BI Publisher links into EBS pages

To add a link to BIP in an Oracle EBS form, create a form function and then assign menus and responsibilities.

For this purpose, log in to Oracle EBS as the system administrator. Select the **System Administrator** responsibility from the responsibility navigator pane on the left, and then follow the steps described in the following subsections.

## Create a form function

**To create a form function**, go to the **Application** menu and select **Function**. The **Form Functions** dialog appears, as shown in the following screenshot:

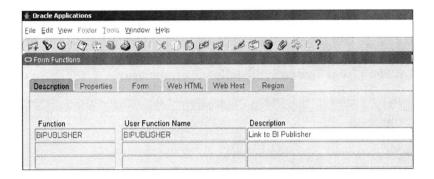

1. In the **Function** field enter the name of the function, for example, **BIPUBLISHER**.

2. Enter the **User function name** field, for example, **BIPUBLISHER**.

3. Enter a description in the corresponding field, for example, **Link to BI Publisher**.

4. Save your changes by clicking on the **Save** button on the toolbar.

5. Select the **Properties** tab and in the **Type** field select **SSWA (Oracle Self Service Web Applications) jsp function** as shown in the following screenshot:

6. Select the **Web HTML** tab and in the **HTML Call** field enter:

    ○ The link to answers is as follows:
      `OracleOasis.jsp?mode=OBIEE&function=Answers`

    ○ The link to Dashboards is as follows:
      `OracleOasis.jsp?mode=OBIEE&function=Dashboard`

7. Save your changes using the **Save** button on the toolbar.

8. Close the **Form Functions** dialog.

# Create a menu

We'll create a menu that invokes the previously created form function in EBS. From the **Application** menu, select **Menu**. Or, if you are already in forms, select **Menus** from the **Top Ten List** as shown in the following screenshot:

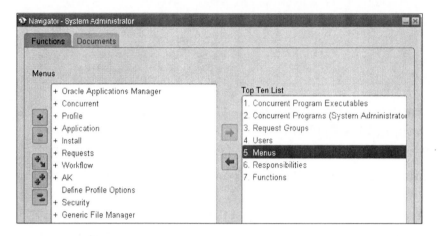

Enter values for the menu's fields as follows:

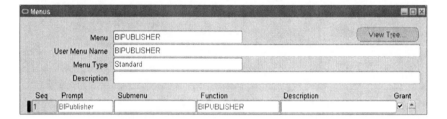

In the **Function** field, enter the name of the function created in the earlier section. The function will be selected by default for the user as it is the only function of the menu.

# Assign the menu to a responsibility

In order to have access to the menu, this must be assigned to an existing or a new responsibility. The necessary steps to be followed to assign the menu to a new responsibility will be described. In order to do this, select **Responsibilities** from the **Top Ten List**. The **Responsibilities** window will be displayed as shown in the following screenshot:

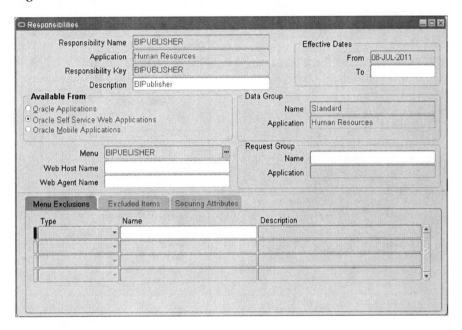

In the **Responsibilities** dialog shown in the preceding screenshot enter the following:

1. **Responsibility name** – for example, BIPUBISHER.
2. **Application** – the application for which you created the menu.
3. **Responsibility Key** – define unique value.
4. **Available From** – select **Oracle Self Service Web Applications**.
5. **Data Group** – enter **Standard** in the **Name** field and the application name in the **Application** field.
6. **Menu** – the name of the menu created in the section before.
7. Save your changes using the **Save** button on the toolbar.
8. Close the **Responsibilities** dialog.

# Assign the responsibility to a user

To assign the responsibility to an existing user, carry out the following steps:

1.  In the **Top Ten List** choose **Users**. The **Users** dialog appears, as shown in the following screenshot:

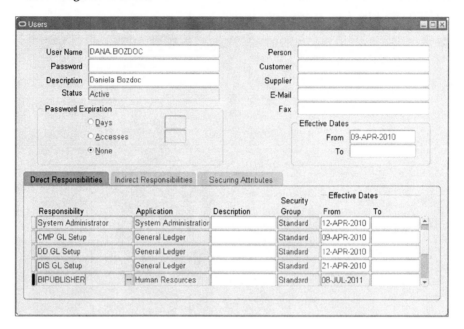

2.  Select the **User Name** to which you want to assign the responsibility.
3.  Add a new row in the **Direct Responsibilities** tab and choose the responsibility you've created.
4.  Enter **Effective Dates**.
5.  Save your changes by clicking on the **Save** button on the toolbar.
6.  Close the **Users** dialog.

# Set up a profile

The URL of the Oracle BI Publisher will be entered as part of a profile. The profile name to set is **FND: Oracle Business Intelligence Suite**. To set this profile value for the previously created responsibility, go to the **Application** menu and select **Profile**. The **Find system Profile Values** dialog will be displayed:

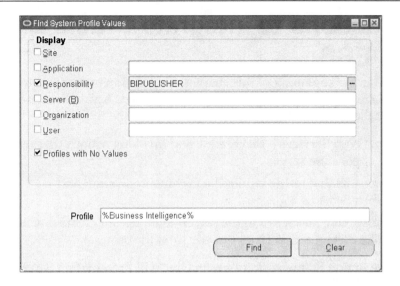

Carry out the following steps:

1. Select **Responsibility**, and then enter the name of the responsibility to which you assigned the menu.

2. In the **Profile** field enter %**Business Intelligence**%.

3. Click on **Find**.

4. In the **System Profile Values** interface, under **Responsibility**, enter the Oracle BI Publisher URL. For example:

   ```
   http://my_server.domain.com:port/xmlpserver
   ```

5. For port, enter the Web server port where Oracle Business Intelligence is running (for example, 9704):

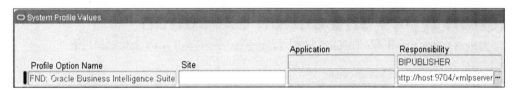

6. Save your changes using the **Save** button on the toolbar.

# Using actions to integrate Oracle BI with Oracle EBS

As mentioned in the beginning of this chapter, the solution to navigate to EBS from BIP exists. To create this link, **Action Framework** is used. Action Framework, a component of the Oracle BI EE architecture, consists of the following:

- **Actions Web Services**—for creating and invoking actions that are deployed in the application server
- Components that reside within the Presentation Server and Scheduler Services
- Action-specific JavaScript in the presentation tier for creating actions and invoking certain action types directly from the browser

To prepare the Action Framework for use in Oracle BI Presentation Services, you must perform the following tasks:

- Configure the Action Framework
- Secure actions
- Set up action targets

## Functionality

The Action Framework provides functionality for creating, managing, and invoking actions. Actions provide functionality to navigate to context and to invoke operations, functions, or processes in external systems. Actions are created and managed in the Oracle BI Presentation Services user interface.

## Action types and action execution

The action types available in Oracle BI EE are categorized into actions that:

- Navigate to related content
- Invoke operations, functions, or processes in external systems

Based on the technology they invoke, actions can be further categorized into actions that invoke URLs or Web services.

The action type **Navigate to E-Business Suite** allows users to navigate from Oracle BI EE to Oracle EBS. The Oracle BI EE session holds the context of the user's Oracle EBS session, including the current Oracle EBS responsibility in the Oracle BI EE session variables.

A Navigate to Oracle E-Business Suite action takes two parameters:

- **Connection Pool**: Contains the name of the BI connection pool that connects to the target EBS environment as defined in the repository. **Oracle EBS 12** in our example.

- **Function**: Contains the name of the target EBS function to which to navigate. The EBS administrator needs to provide the target function ID. For example, use **BIPUBLISHER** — the function ID we've created in this chapter.

To invoke a Navigate to EBS action, the user must have privileges to execute direct database requests against the EBS connection pool. Also, the target EBS function must be accessible from the user's current EBS.

This short introduction will help you to figure out how this process works, but it is a little more complicated to set up actions. So let's leave this task to the Oracle BI system administrator.

# Summary

At the end of this chapter you should be able to set up Oracle BI to use Oracle EBS security to authenticate users, and you should have an idea about what Action Framework is and what action type you should use to integrate Oracle BI with Oracle EBS.

You must have realized by now that you have all the reasons, including the EBS integration to use or upgrade to BIP 11g. However, there is another category of reports that deserve our attention, **Oracle reports**. Oracle reports and their migration to BIP will be the main topic of *Appendix B, Migrating Oracle Reports to BI Publisher*.

# A
# Report Translations

Providing a translation for a report is an important part of the report layout design in cases of foreign customers, foreign providers, or any other document exchange with a foreign partner. It is important in countries using English language too.

This chapter proposes a walkthrough for all the translation techniques that BI Publisher offers, including:

- Translation file
- Step by step translations
- Locale selection logic

## Translation file

The translation file, named XLIFF, is generated either inside BI Publisher or from MS Word using the Template Builder add-on for Word.

The **XML Localization Interchange file Format (XLIFF)** is the standard format used by localization providers.

In the following image, you can see the elements of an XLIFF file structure. Open the XLIFF file in a browser to get a similar view of the **DOM (Document Object Model)** structure. The most important tags, you will be working with in the translation process, are as follows:

- `<file>`
- `<source>`
- `<target>`

This is not a translated version of an XLIFF file—the `<source>` and `<target>` tags have identical content, as shown in the following screenshot:

```xml
<?xml version="1.0" encoding="utf-8" ?>
- <xliff version="1.0">
  - <file source-language="en" target-language="en" datatype="xml" product-version="11.1.1.3.0" product-name="BI
      Publisher">
    - <body>
      - <trans-unit id="xdo#%2F%7Eweblogic%2FDrafts%2FDraft+-+Apr+24+2011+10-01-
          58+PM.xdo#tmp_books.xpt">
          <source>books</source>
          <target>books</target>
        </trans-unit>
      - <trans-unit id="xpt#%2F%7Eweblogic%2FDrafts%2FDraft+-+Apr+24+2011+10-01-
          58+PM.xdo#books.xpt#23">
          <source>[&0][&1]Report Title[&1] [&0]</source>
          <target>[&0][&1]Report Title[&1] [&0]</target>
        </trans-unit>
      - <trans-unit id="xpt#%2F%7Eweblogic%2FDrafts%2FDraft+-+Apr+24+2011+10-01-
          58+PM.xdo#books.xpt#24">
          <source>[&0][&1]Proprietary and Confidential[&1][&0][&2][&2]</source>
          <target>[&0][&1]Proprietary and Confidential[&1][&0][&2][&2]</target>
        </trans-unit>
```

The circumstances under which BI Publisher is used depends on the user's need, and business partners, there are more techniques available in BI Publisher.

Check out the next section to get a better understanding of the way the XLIFF file is used.

# Catalog translation

You can use this type of translation when you want all the objects that BI Publisher includes to be translated. This feature allows translation of the following:

- Report layouts
- Catalog object descriptions
- Report parameter's names
- Data display names

It is a good choice to use catalog translation when the users working with BI Publisher use a language other than English. Users viewing the catalog will see the item translations appropriate for the **UI Language** and report translations appropriate for the **Report Locale** they selected in their My Account preferences.

On the home page of BI Publisher, click on the **My Account** link found under your username, to set your preferences. This is shown in the following screenshot:

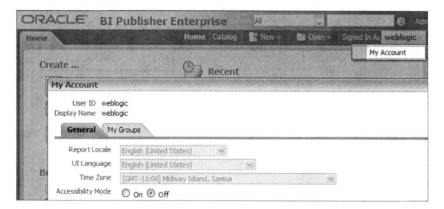

Your preferences may be inherited from another Oracle product. In this case, you cannot update your preferences from within BI Publisher. This is one of the situations captured in the preceding image.

 When BI Publisher is integrated with Oracle BIEE, BI Publisher catalog translation is ignored.

For a catalog translation perform the following steps:

1. In BI Publisher, open the catalog and select the folder to be translated.

2. Click on the **Translation** icon shown in the following screenshot and select the **Export XLIFF** menu option.

3. Save the .xlf file in a folder of your choice:

4. Open the XLIFF file using a text editor. It will look like the following screenshot:

```
<?xml version = '1.0' encoding = 'utf-8'?>
<xliff version="1.0">
   <file source-language="en" target-language="ro" datatype="xml"
      <body>
         <trans-unit id="xdo#%2F%7Eweblogic%2FDrafts%2FDraft+-+Ap
            <source>books</source>
            <target>books</target>
         </trans-unit>
         <trans-unit id="xpt#%2F%7Eweblogic%2FDrafts%2FDraft+-+Ap
            <source>[&amp;0][&amp;1]Report Title[&amp;1]
            <target>[&amp;0][&amp;1]Report Title[&amp;1]
         </trans-unit>
```

5. Change the `target-language` attribute of the `<file>` tag with the target language code.

 Only **en** is available for the source language.

6. Provide a translation for the text contained by the `<source>` tags. You have to enter the translation between the corresponding `<target>` tags.

   This file also contains object names and not only text strings contained by these objects, as you can see in the following screenshot:

```
<trans-unit id="catalog#%2F%7Eweblogic%2FDrafts#Library.xdo">
   <source>Library</source>
   <target>Biblioteca</target>
</trans-unit>
<trans-unit id="catalog#%2F%7Eweblogic%2FDrafts#Product+sales.xdo">
   <source>Product sales</source>
   <target>Vanzari</target>
</trans-unit>
<trans-unit id="catalog#%2F%7Eweblogic%2FDrafts#Readers+20110418.xdo">
   <source>Readers 20110418</source>
   <target>Cititori 20110418</target>
</trans-unit>
```

   Notice that opening the file in MS Word 2007—as shown in the following image—will generate a simplified version, not allowing attribute changing or viewing. But at the same time, simpler is better when you only need `<source>` and `<target>` tags to enter the translation and your work will be ready in no time:

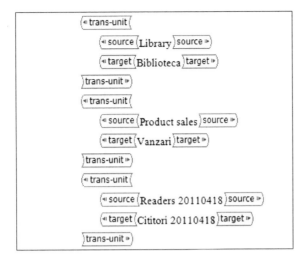

7.  Upload the translated file back to BI Publisher.

    Click on the **Translation** icon and go to the **Import XLIFF** menu option. This will open the **Upload** dialog window. Browse for the file containing the catalog translation and click on **Upload**:

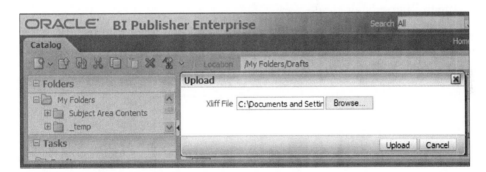

# File translation

At a lower level than catalog translation, file translation allows you to translate only specific objects from the BI Publisher catalog. The objects you can translate are as follows:

*   RTF templates
*   Style templates
*   Subtemplates
*   BI Publisher templates (.XPT)

Using this technique, you will be able to provide translations in circumstances where the users want to consult only some reports in another language, or they want to send documents to the partners in different languages.

The way file translation is actually realized depends on another factor: whether the translated template needs another layout than the original template or not. In the first case, you must create another localized template, in the second case you'll use an XLIFF file, allowing you to translate only the text strings of the template.

This section will present concrete steps to follow in order to generate report translation for the cases listed as follows:

- Same layout using BIP
- Same layout using Template Builder for Word
- Different layouts

## Same layout using BIP

Let's assume first that you only need the text strings of the layout template to be translated. In this case, follow the steps:

1. Open BI Publisher catalog.
2. Click on the **Edit** link under the report name you want to translate.
3. Click on the **Properties** link under the report layout to be translated, as shown in the following screenshot:

4.  This will open the **Properties** page shown below:

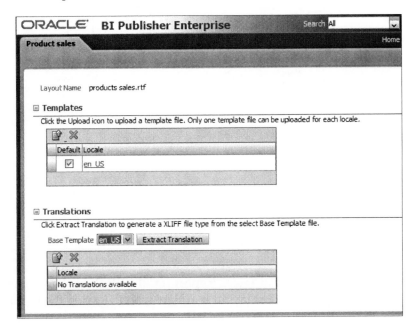

5.  Click on **Extract translation** to trigger the process that generates the XLIFF file.

6.  Save the XLIFF file to a folder of your choice.

7.  Update the XLIFF file by providing text between the `<target>` tags corresponding to the translated text from the `<source>` tags as you can see in the following screenshot:

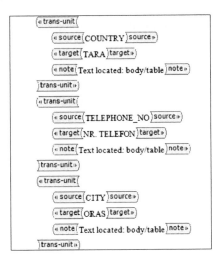

8. Click on the **Upload** icon in the **Translations** section to get your translated XLIFF file into BIP:

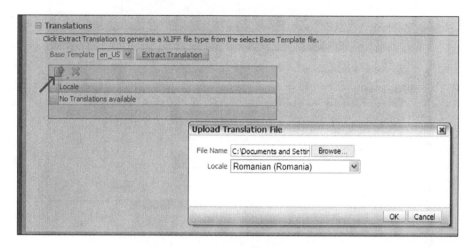

In this way, when choosing **Romanian** as **Report Locale**, BI Publisher will apply the translation for this particular report layout template when viewing the report.

# Same layout using Template Builder for Word

As mentioned earlier, the Template Builder for Word can be used to generate the XLIFF file. The steps required in this case are as follows:

1. Open the RTF layout template file using Word.
2. Go to the **Translation | Extract Text...** menu option on the toolbar. This will generate the XLIFF file.
3. Save the XLIFF file in a folder of your choice using the `.xlf` extension.
4. Translate the text between the `<target>` tags providing translation for the text between the `<source>` tags, and save your work:

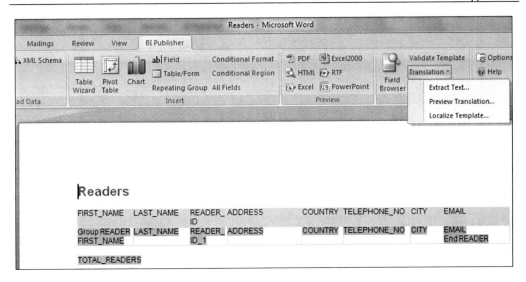

5. Go to the **Translation | Preview Translation...** menu option on the toolbar and choose the modified file to see the result, as shown in the following screenshot:

## Cititori

| PRENUME | NUME | ID CITITOR | ADRESA | TARA | NR. TELEFON | ORAS | EMAIL |
|---------|------|-----------|--------|------|-------------|------|-------|
| Crina | Istrate | 3 | Str. Raului Nr.35 | HU | 932-328-3277 | Budapest | crina_istrate@yahoo.com |
| Maria | Coman | 4 | Str. Islazului Nr.7 | HU | 0932-397-327 | Budapest | maria_coman@yahoo.com |
| Sofia | Ghis | 5 | Str. Al.Borza Nr.8 | HU | 0388-328-32 | Budapest | sofia_chis@gmail.com |

A good result means that your XLIFF file is correct and now you can proceed to upload it into BIP.

6. In BIP, click on the **Upload** icon in the **Translations** section, and browse for the saved XLIFF file in order to get your translation file into BIP.

# Different layouts

Here are the steps to follow when different layouts are needed for different languages:

1. Design a brand new layout for your report. For example, here the columns have a different order than those in the original layout template and a column is missing. At the same time, the template text strings are translated:

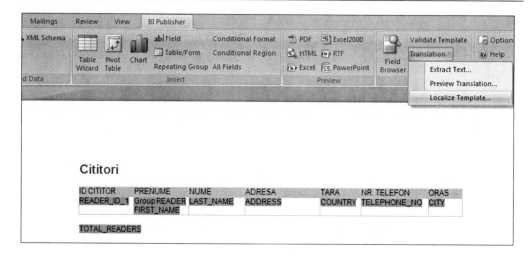

 You can make changes to the translated template permanently by clicking on the **Translation | Localize Template...** menu option on the toolbar. In this way, when only minor changes are necessary, you don't need to start your new layout design from scratch (or worst, with a blank document).

2. Upload the template into BIP. Be careful to choose the appropriate **Locale** for your template, as shown in the following screenshot:

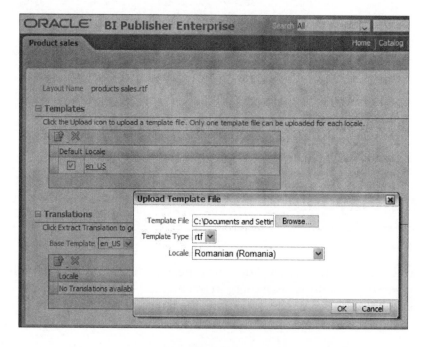

# Locale selection logic

**My Account** interface allows you to choose a **Report Locale** to determine which RTF file, and then which XLIFF file, will be used. If an exact match on language-territory is not found, BI Publisher will try to match on the basis of language only. For example, you have a report template called `Sales.rtf` uploaded for the ro-RO locale. BI Publisher will search the RTF template and translation files like this:

- Sales.rtf (ro_RO)
- Sales.xlf (ro_RO)
- Sales.rtf (ro)
- Sales.xlf (ro)
- Sales.rtf (default)

For situations such as different territories, it is recommended that we provide an RTF or XLF file named for the language only. Suppose that you have:

- Sales.rtf (**en_UK**)
- Sales.xlf (**en_UK**)
- Sales.rtf (**default**)

In this case, when BIP looks for **en_CA** and this locale is not found, the **default** template will be applied and not the template including **en** as language. To avoid this, include only `Sales_en.rtf` or `Sales_en.xlf` for the language. For this you need to upload the mentioned files (`Sales_en.rtf` or `Sales_en.xlf`) selecting only the language for the **Locale**, as shown in the following screenshot:

# Summary

You should now be familiar with all kinds of report translations, both from the theoretical and practical point of view. The step-by-step examples were provided to identify the differences between the techniques BI Publisher offers and the circumstances for each of them to be used. We saw that there are many cases in which report translations are used, but there is not much effort required when following step-by-step instructions.

# B

# Migrating Oracle Reports to BI Publisher

The advantages presented throughout the previous chapters might have convinced you to use BI Publisher to design your reports. But why not use the same capabilities on your old Oracle Reports? Beginning with release 10.1.3.3, BI Publisher introduces the ability to convert Oracle Reports to BI Publisher.

In this chapter, we will see the following:

- Converting Oracle Reports to BI Publisher prerequisites
- Conversion steps

## Prerequisites

To start report conversion, you need to have the following installed on your computer:

- Oracle Reports Designer
- BI Publisher
- JDK

## Installing Oracle Reports Designer

You need to install Oracle Reports Designer only if your Oracle Reports are not already in XML format.

We will use version 10.1.2.0.2 for this example. To install this version follow the steps given here:

1. Download Oracle Developer Suite 10g from:

   ```
   http://www.oracle.com/technology/software/products/ids/
   index.html
   ```

2. Run the setup process providing the parameters, as described in the following screenshot:

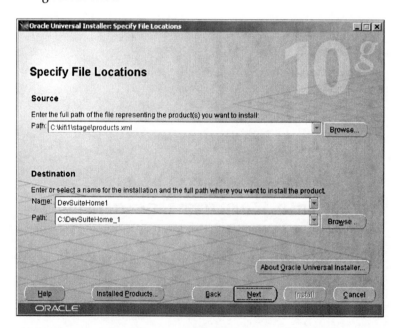

3. Select the **Complete** option for **Select Installation Type**, as shown in the following screenshot:

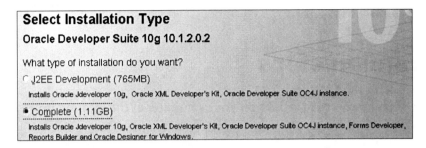

After completing the installation, you should be able to run Oracle Reports Designer from the menu link, as shown in the following screenshot:

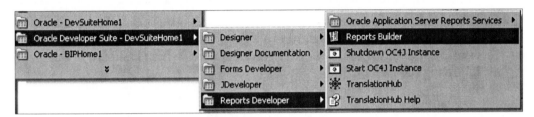

# Installing BI Publisher

You can skip this step if you are using Oracle EBS.

Download BI Publisher 10.1.3.4 release from:

http://www.oracle.com/technetwork/middleware/bi-publisher/downloads/index.html

Now, follow the setup process to install the BI Publisher.

# Installing JDK

The conversion utility requires JDK version 1.1.8 or later.

Test your currently installed version, as shown in the following screenshot:

```
C:\WINDOWS\system32\cmd.exe
Microsoft Windows XP [Version 5.1.2600]
(C) Copyright 1985-2001 Microsoft Corp.

C:\Program Files\Java\jre6\bin>java -version
java version "1.6.0_24"
Java(TM) SE Runtime Environment (build 1.6.0_24-b07)
Java HotSpot(TM) Client VM (build 19.1-b02, mixed mode, sharing)
```

In case your version does not satisfy the requirements, get the latest version from:

`http://www.oracle.com/technetwork/java/javase/downloads/jdk-6u26-download-400750.html`

# Conversion steps

1.  Search for the `aolj.jar`, `collections.jar`, `xdocore.jar`, and `xmlparserv2-904.jar` files on your computer at the location provided in the following URL:

    `C:\OraHome_1\oc4j_bi\j2ee\home\applications\xmlpserver\`
    `xmlpserver\WEB-INF\lib`

    You may also find these libraries, or the corresponding classes, under JAVA_ TOP (this is a folder on the Oracle Application middle-tier machine) if you are using Oracle EBS.

2.  Copy the files mentioned before to a location of your choice. In this example, the `C:\oracle\convert` folder is used, which is shown in the following screenshot:

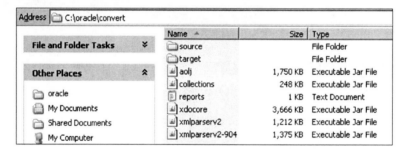

3.  Copy the Oracle Reports that have to be converted into the `source` folder.

4. Run Oracle Reports Builder and go to the **File Conversion** tool. Skip this step if your reports are already in the XML format, as shown in the following screenshot:

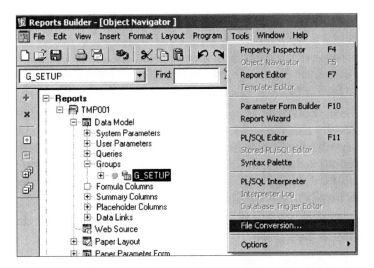

Browse for your `.rdf` file in the **Source** field and choose **Report XML File (XML)** as the **Destination Type**, as shown in the following screenshot:

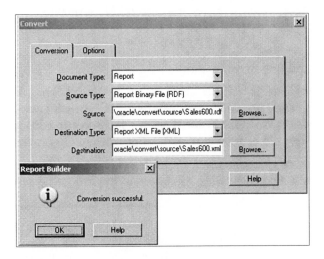

Once done, a **Conversion successful** message is displayed, as shown in the preceding screenshot.

6. Now, run the conversion utility.

BIPBatchConversion is the utility to migrate reports from Oracle Reports to BI Publisher. It takes the following parameters:

- `source` (required): Source directory for Oracle Reports files. All reports must be in the same format, that is, either RDF or XML.

- `target` (required): Target directory to create Oracle BI Publisher report objects. This includes the Oracle BI Publisher Report file (`.xdo`), the layout template file (`.rtf`), the PL/SQL package, and the log file.

- `oraclehome` (optional): If your reports are in Oracle Reports XML format, do not specify this parameter. If your reports are not in Oracle Reports XML format, specify the Oracle home path where Oracle Report Designer (9i or later version) is installed. Refer to the *Install Oracle Reports Designer* section for this. BIPBatchMigration assumes that `rwconverter` is contained in the `bin` directory beneath the Oracle Home path.

- `debug` (optional): To run the utility in debug mode and write debug statements to the log file.

We already converted our reports to XML format, so the `oraclehome` parameter won't be needed in this case.

 Leave the reports only in XML format in the `source` folder.

The command line in our example is:

C:\ "Program files"\Java\jre6\bin\java -classpath C:\oracle\convert\xdo-core.jar; C:\oracle\convert \collections.zip; C:\oracle\convert\aolj.jar; C:\ oracle\convert \xmlparserv2-904.jar oracle.apps.xdo.rdfparser.BIPBatchCon-version -source C:\oracle\convert\source -target C:\oracle\convert\target

Output files are generated in a folder for each report. In our case, the folder `Sales600` contains these files, as shown in the following screenshot:

- `Sales600.xdo`: Report definition file that includes the Data Model. This file is not needed for EBS users.
- `Sales600_template.xml`: It is a Data Template. This is not required for Oracle BI Publisher Enterprise users because the data template is embedded in the `.xdo` file.
- `Sales600S.pls`: This is the default PL/SQL package.
- `Sales600B.pls`: This is the default PL/SQL package body.
- `Sales600.rtf`: This is the RTF Layout Template.
- `Sales600.log`: This is a log file.
- `Sales600_LOV.xml`: This is a list of values file.

7. Load the PL/SQL package into the database.

   Create the package and the package body from the `.pls` files, as shown in the following command lines:

   SQL> @C:\oracle\convert]target\Sales600\Sales600S.pls

   SQL> @C:\oracle\convert]target\Sales600\Sales600B.pls

8. Upload the report to the Oracle BI Publisher repository.

   First copy the files to the repository and then refresh the repository metadata. For this, log on to Oracle BI Publisher with administrator privileges, go to the **Admin** page, and select **Refresh Metadata** from the **System Maintenance** section, as shown in the following screenshot:

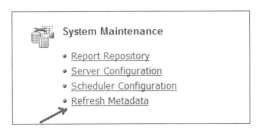

9. Test the report and check the conversion log files to identify any manual modifications needed to complete the conversion.

When converting a complex Oracle Reports report, the Data Template or PL/SQL may contain minor errors and require manual correction. For example, the conversion utility does not convert any PL/SQL format trigger logic present in the report. Instead the conversion utility writes all the format trigger code to a log file. You will need to implement any corresponding PL/SQL logic as XSL code. Refer to *Appendix C, Debugging Oracle Reports to BIP Migration*, for a more comprehensive example.

# Summary

Going through the steps mentioned in this chapter should have made you understand the process of converting Oracle Reports to BI Publisher, that is, how to meet the prerequisites and the actual conversion steps. The main purpose is to work on the same platform when designing reports and to take advantage of all the beautiful features that BI Publisher offers.

*Appendic C, Debugging Oracle Reports to BIP Migration*, will deal with an error that frequently occurs in the Oracle Reports to BIP migration process.

# C
# Debugging Oracle Reports to BIP Migration

In *Appendix B, Migrating Oracle Reports to BI Publisher*, we went through the necessary steps involved in converting Oracle Reports to BI Publisher. There were a few cases mentioned, in which manual correction was needed after the conversion of a complex Oracle Reports report to BIP. Here, we will have described one of those cases.

## Finding the error

In this case, the conversion utility does not convert a PL/SQL format trigger logic present in the report:

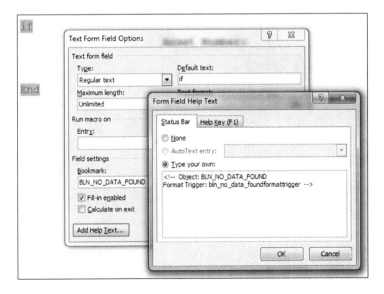

The fields highlighted in red are added in the template to help you quickly indentify the problem. The missing objects are mentioned in the **Form Field Help Text** dialog window, as you can see in the preceding screenshot.

# The log file

A log file named as your template will show the code behind the missing objects. For our case we will have:

```
The following format triggers which are the part of RDF,
has not been supported in this Template:
-----------------------------------------------------------
 Object Name : BLN_NO_DATA_FOUND
 Object Type : frame
===========================================================
PL/Sql code
       function BLN_NO_DATA_FOUND
FormatTrigger return boolean is
begin
RETURN(:C_count = 0);  return (TRUE);
end;
-----------------------------------------------------------
```

# Correcting the error

In order to correct an error, all we have to do is to rewrite the trigger and the XLS_FO. The following are the alternatives depending on the XML structure:

- In the case the element is not present:

    ```
    <?if:not(element_name)?>
    ```

    (desired behavior)

    ```
    <?end if?>
    ```

- The element is present and the value is not null:

    ```
    <?if:element_name!=?>
    ```

    (desired behavior)

    ```
    <?end if?>
    ```

- The element is present, but is null:

```
<?if:element_name and element_name=""?>
```

(desired behavior)

```
<?end if?>
```

As the first case is the suitable match in this example, the XSL-FO code will
be as follows:

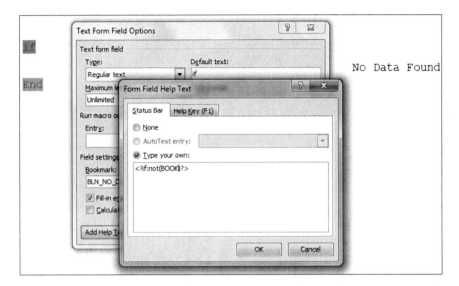

According to your data, many other more or less complicated situations can be
encountered. But you have a lot of clues helping you to solve the case. Finally, you
will have your report converted into BIP.

# D
# Glossary

## A

**Accessibility**: The Template Builder provides an accessibility checker to check the template for features to enhance the accessibility of the report, for report consumers who may need assistive technologies to view the report.

**Action Framework**: A component of the Oracle BI EE architecture, consisting of:

- Actions Web Services for creating and invoking actions that are deployed in the application server
- Components that reside within the Presentation Server and Scheduler Services
- Actions-specific JavaScript in the presentation tier for creating actions and invoking certain action types directly from the browser

**Analyzer for Excel**: A BIP tool that enables:

- The export of the results of the report query to an Excel spreadsheet
- To log in to BI Publisher Enterprise from Excel to refresh data, apply new Parameters, and apply a Template to the report data
- To create Excel Templates and upload them to the BI Publisher server
- To access and run reports from an Excel session

# B

**Business Intelligence Suite Enterprise Edition Plus (BI EE)**: A comprehensive suite of enterprise Oracle BI products, delivering the full range of BI capabilities including interactive dashboards, full ad hoc proactive intelligence and alerts, enterprise and financial reporting, real-time predictive intelligence, disconnected analytics, and more.

**BI Publisher (BIP)**: Formerly known as Oracle XML Publisher, BIP is Oracle's reporting XML based technology, which generates highly formatted data output using multiple data sources.

**Bursting**: A process of splitting data into blocks. For each block of the data, a separate document is generated and delivered to one or more destinations.

**Business Intelligence (BI)**: This is the process of transforming data gathered from all business data sources into decision support business information. BI technologies provide historical, current, and predictive views of business operations. Common functions of business intelligence technologies are reporting, online analytical processing, analytics, data mining, process mining, business performance management, benchmarking, text mining, and predictive analytics.

**Business performance management**: A set of management and analytic processes that enables the management of an organization's performance to achieve one or more pre-selected goals.

# C

**Cache**: A component that temporarily and transparently stores data so that future requests for that data can be served faster. The data that is stored within a cache might be values that have been computed earlier or duplicates of original values that are stored elsewhere.

**Catalog**: The structure of folders containing all the elements created in BI Publisher

# D

**Data mining**: The process of discovering new patterns from large Data Sets involving methods from statistics and artificial intelligence, but also database management.

**Data Model**: A BIP concept, including a set of components needed to generate an XML file at runtime as a Data Source for a BIP report.

**Data Model editor**: Enables the BIP tools to choose various types of Data Sources, and to build the desired model and structure of data.

**Data Template**: Defines the BIP layout format. The Data Template can be designed using Microsoft Word, Adobe Acrobat, Microsoft Excel (standalone version), Adobe Flash (standalone version), and Oracle BI Publisher's own layout editor.

**Data warehouse (DW)**: A database used for reporting and analysis. The data stored in the warehouse is uploaded from the operational systems. The data may pass through an operational data store for additional operations before it is used in the data warehouse for reporting.

**Document Object Model (DOM)**: A cross-platform and language-independent convention for representing and interacting with objects in HTML, XHTML, and XML documents.

# E

**eText Templates**: They are specialized RTF Templates for constructing Electronic Funds Transfer (EFT) and Electronic Data Interchange (EDI) transaction files.

**E-Business Suite (EBS)**: Oracle Corporation's E-Business Suite consists of a collection of Enterprise Resource Planning (ERP), Customer Relationship Management (CRM), and Supply-Chain Management (SCM) computer applications either developed by, or acquired by, Oracle.

**Enterprise Reporting**: A process that involves querying data sources with different logical models to produce a human readable report.

**Entity**: Something that has a distinct, separate existence, although it need not be a material existence. In particular, abstractions and legal fictions are usually regarded as entities. In general, there is also no presumption that an entity is animate.

**ETL (extract, transform, load)**: A process in database usage and especially in data warehousing that involves:

- Extracting data from outside sources
- Transforming it to fit operational needs (which can include quality levels)
- Loading it into the end target (database or data warehouse)

**Event Triggers**: They are the equivalent of Report triggers from the Data Template in BIP 10g. A trigger can be set to be fired before or after the completion of the report. This will call one or more database functions.

**Excel Template**: It is the report layout that you design in Microsoft Excel for retrieving and formatting your enterprise reporting data in Excel.

# F

**Filter**: Refines the displayed items by a condition. This is a powerful feature that enables you to display only desired elements in your table (filter them) without having to perform additional coding.

**Flash Template**: A template designed using Adobe Flash Player.

**Flexfield**: In an Oracle environment, a Flexfield is a database field that has flexibility built into it, so that users can define reporting structures that are relevant to their specific organizations. Two types of flexfields are provided:

- Key flexfields, which are required to record key data elements in Oracle applications
- Descriptive flexfields, which are user-defined and record data elements that aren't automatically provided

# G

**Group**: In a Layout Template context, for each occurrence of a group element, the included fields are displayed.

# H

**HTML (HyperText Markup Language)**: It is the predominant markup language for web pages. HTML elements are the basic building-blocks of webpages.

# J

**Java**: A programming language originally developed by James Gosling at Sun Microsystems. It is a general-purpose, concurrent, class-based, object-oriented language that is specifically designed to have as few implementation dependencies as possible.

**Java DataBase Connectivity (JDBC)**: An API (Application Programming Interface) for the Java programming language that defines how a client may access a database.

**Java Naming and Directory Interface (JNDI)**: It is a Java API for a directory service that allows Java software clients to discover and look up data and objects via a name.

# L

**Layout**: Defines how the data is presented in the report. A layout consists of a template file and a set of properties for rendering the template file.

**Lightweight Directory Access Protocol (LDAP)**: An application protocol for accessing and maintaining distributed directory information services over an Internet Protocol (IP) network.

**Locale**: A set of parameters that defines the user's language, country, and any special variant preferences that the user wants to see in their user interface. Usually a locale identifier consists of at least a language identifier and a region identifier.

**Localizing a template**: Creates a template to be used for a specific language.

# M

**Markup**: You add a markup to create the mapping between your layout and the XML file, and to include features that cannot be represented directly in your format. The most basic markup elements are placeholders used to define the XML data elements, and groups used to define the repeating elements.

# N

**Namespace**: Namespaces provide a simple method for qualifying element and attribute names used in Extensible Markup Language documents by associating them with namespaces identified by URI references

# O

**OLAP (Online Analytical Processing)**: An approach to swiftly answer Multi-dimensional Analytical (MDA) queries. OLAP tools enable users to interactively analyze multi-dimensional data from multiple perspectives.

**Online Analyzer**: Enables you to create ad hoc pivot views of your data. In a pivot table structure, you can drag-and-drop data elements, which can be afterwards arranged, filtered, and summarized.

**Oracle Reports**: A tool for developing reports against data stored in an Oracle database. Oracle Reports consists of Oracle Reports Developer (a component of the Oracle Developer Suite) and Oracle Application Server Reports Services (a component of the Oracle Application Server).

# P

**PDF (Portable Document Format)**: An open standard for document exchange. This file format created by Adobe Systems in 1993 is used for representing documents in a manner independent of application software, hardware, and operating systems.

**PDF Templates**: They are templates designed using Adobe Acrobat by applying BI Publisher markup to an existing PDF document.

**PDFZ (Zipped PDF)**: The output file of a report is split into multiple files generated in one zip file.

**Pivot table**: Provides views of multidimensional data in a tabular format. It supports multiple measures and dimensions, and subtotals at all levels.

**Placeholder**: This is the template report field of the XML element.

**Predictive analytics**: Encompasses a variety of statistical techniques from modeling, data mining, and game theory that analyze current and historical facts to make predictions about future events.

# R

**Report job**: A BIP component used to schedule the reports for delivery.

**Repository Creation Utility (RCU)**: A graphical and CLI (Command Line Interface) based tool, used to create and manage Oracle Fusion Middleware database schemas.

**Rich Text Format (RTF)**: A specification used by common word processing applications, including Microsoft Word.

# S

**SQL (Structured Query Language)**: A database computer declarative language designed for managing data in Relational Database Management Systems (RDBMS).

**Style templates**: Templates applied to RTF layouts to keep the company identity intact across all company reports

**Sub-templates**: RTF or XSL files used for defining a reusable formatting functionality in BI Publisher.

# T

**Tag**: Elements that are used to classify and describe data in an XML document so that the data becomes uniquely identifiable.

**Template**: A pre-developed page layout in electronic or paper media used to make new pages with a similar design, pattern, or style.

**Template Builder for Word**: Plugin provided by BIP that assists in RTF Template design and enables a connection to BIP to access data and upload templates directly from Word.

**Translation file**: A named XLIFF, is the standard format used by localization providers generated either inside BI Publisher or from MS Word using the Template Builder for Word.

**Trigger**: A procedural code that is automatically executed in response to certain events on a particular table or view in a database. The trigger is mostly used for keeping the integrity of the information on the database.

# U

**Upgrade assistant utility**: An Oracle tool used to upgrade the repository and Web Catalogs when moving from BIP 10g to 11g.

# X

**XML (Extensible Markup Language)**: A set of rules for encoding documents in machine-readable format. It is defined in the XML 1.0 Specification produced by the W3C, and several other related specifications, all gratis open standards.

**XML Localization Interchange File Format** (XLIFF): The standard format used by localization providers.

**XML Publisher**: An Oracle reporting technology, which is the previous version of BI Publisher.

**XPT**: A file extension used for BIP layout editor templates, designed using a pure web based layout editor offered starting with the 11g release.

**XSL (Extensible Stylesheet Language)**: Refers to a family of languages used to transform and render XML documents.

**XSL-FO (XSL Formatting Objects)**: A markup language for XML document format which is most often used to generate PDFs.

# Z

**ZIP**: A data compression and archive format. A ZIP file contains one or more files that have been compressed, to reduce file size, or stored as is. The ZIP file format permits a number of compression algorithms.

**Zipped PDF**: A feature of BI Publisher to split a large PDF output file into a smaller one, manage more files, while still maintaining the integrity of the report as one logical unit.

# Index

examples 60
output types 60
parameters 30

# C

caching tab, Report Properties 142
catalog translation
  about 198-201
  features 198
chart, insert template elements 129
charts
  creating 112
code view, data set structure 47
components, Oracle BI Publisher 11g
  data query 20
  data template 20
  report definition 20
  report jobs 20
conditional region, insert
      template elements 130
connection pool
  creating 181, 183
conversion log files
  checking 215
conversion steps, Oracle Reports 212, 213
Create Report Interface 107, 123, 173
CSV 60, 148
currency format tab, Report Properties 144

# D

database object, creating 181
data definition 14
Data Model
  about 37
  building 14, 15
  components 37
  editor interface 37
Data Model editor
  about 23
  bursting 60
  data sets 39
  data structure builder 45
  event triggers 56
  flexfields 56, 57
  List of Values (LOVs) 57, 58
  multiple report characteristics 37

parameters 59
Data Model editor interface
  about 37, 38, 161
  elements, required for report 38
  functionality 38
data modelling 52-55
Data Model, simple report example
  creating 161-168
Data Model structure
  about 81
  creating, for report 83
  data sets, adding 69, 71
Data query 15, 20
data, Report Viewer 148
Data Set parameters
  about 79
  actions 80
  interface, for HTTP Data Set 79
  interface, for Microsoft Excel file data set
      type 80
data sets, Data Model editor
  about 39, 63
  adding, to data structure 39
  data modelling 52-55
  data set types 39
  new data model, creating 48, 49
  query structure, building 50, 51
  XML output, getting 55
Data Sets links
  creating 73
  element-level link 73
  group-level link 74
data set structure
  building 45
data sets types, Data Model editor
  about 63
  HTTP 63
  LDAP Query 63
  MDX Query 63
  Microsoft Excel file 44, 63
  Oracle BI analysis 43
  Oracle BI Analysis 63
  Oracle BI Discoverer 63
  Query Builder interface 40
  SQL query 40
  View Object 63
  Web Service 63

reports, translating 178, 179
source parameter **214**
**SQL Query Data Set**
  configuring 40
**SQL Query statements 78**
**static toolbar, BI Publisher Template 87**
**structure view, data set structure 46**
**Style Templates 19**
**Subtemplate 18**
**sub-templates**
  managing 18

# T

**tabbed toolbar, BI Publisher Template 87**
**Table/Form option, insert template**
       **elements 131**
**target parameter 214**
**template**
  validating 132, 133
**Template Builder**
  installing, for Word 122
  template, validating 132, 133
  translations 133-135
**Template Builder for Word 88**
**Template Builder, for Word**
  about 26
  using 26, 27
**template elements**
  modifying 132
**template types**
  eText Template 103
  Flash Template 103
  PDF Template 101
**Text elements**
  settings 110, 111
**text field, insert template elements 127, 128**

**Text Field Properties dialog 103**
**Tooltip field 103**
**translation file, report translations**
  about 197
  XLIFF file 197
**translation techniques 197**

# U

**upgrade assistant utility 34**

# W

**web-based layout editor 17**

# X

**XLIFF file**
  about 197
  structure 197
**XML 60**
**XML file, data set types 43**
**XML Localization Interchange file Format**
      **file.** *See* **XLIFF file**
**XML output**
  getting 55
**XPT format 107**
**XSLFO 60**
**XSL-FO Stylesheet 97**
**XSL-FO template 144**
**XSL Stylesheet Template**
  about 95
  applying 95-100

# Z

**zipped PDF.** *See* **PDFZ**

**Thank you for buying**
# Oracle BI Publisher 11g:
# A Practical Guide to Enterprise Reporting

## About Packt Publishing

Packt, pronounced 'packed', published its first book "Mastering phpMyAdmin for Effective MySQL Management" in April 2004 and subsequently continued to specialize in publishing highly focused books on specific technologies and solutions.

Our books and publications share the experiences of your fellow IT professionals in adapting and customizing today's systems, applications, and frameworks. Our solution based books give you the knowledge and power to customize the software and technologies you're using to get the job done. Packt books are more specific and less general than the IT books you have seen in the past. Our unique business model allows us to bring you more focused information, giving you more of what you need to know, and less of what you don't.

Packt is a modern, yet unique publishing company, which focuses on producing quality, cutting-edge books for communities of developers, administrators, and newbies alike. For more information, please visit our website: www.packtpub.com.

## About Packt Enterprise

In 2010, Packt launched two new brands, Packt Enterprise and Packt Open Source, in order to continue its focus on specialization. This book is part of the Packt Enterprise brand, home to books published on enterprise software – software created by major vendors, including (but not limited to) IBM, Microsoft and Oracle, often for use in other corporations. Its titles will offer information relevant to a range of users of this software, including administrators, developers, architects, and end users.

## Writing for Packt

We welcome all inquiries from people who are interested in authoring. Book proposals should be sent to author@packtpub.com. If your book idea is still at an early stage and you would like to discuss it first before writing a formal book proposal, contact us; one of our commissioning editors will get in touch with you.

We're not just looking for published authors; if you have strong technical skills but no writing experience, our experienced editors can help you develop a writing career, or simply get some additional reward for your expertise.

## Oracle Business Intelligence : The Condensed Guide to Analysis and Reporting

ISBN: 978-1-84968-118-6        Paperback: 184 pages

A fast track guide to uncovering the analytical power of Oracle Business Intelligence: Analytic SQL, Oracle Discoverer, Oracle Reports, and Oracle Warehouse Builder.

1. Install, configure, and deploy the components included in Oracle Business Intelligence Suite (SE)

2. Gain a comprehensive overview of components and features of the Oracle Business Intelligence package

3. Leverage the computational power of Oracle Database

## The Business Analyst's Guide to Oracle Hyperion Interactive Reporting 11

ISBN: 978-1-84968-036-3        Paperback: 232 pages

Quickly master this powerful business intelligence product

1. Get to grips with the most important, frequently used, and advanced features of Oracle Hyperion Interactive Reporting 11

2. A step-by-step Oracle Hyperion training guide packed with screenshots and clear explanations

3. Explore the features of Hyperion dashboards, reports, pivots, and charts

Please check **www.PacktPub.com** for information on our titles

**Oracle Hyperion Interactive
Reporting 11 Expert Guide**

Learn Advanced Dashboards, JavaScript, Computations,
and Special Topics from the Experts

Edward J. Cody
Emily M. Vose

# Oracle Hyperion Interactive Reporting 11 Expert Guide

ISBN: 978-1-84968-314-2          Paperback: 250 pages

Learn Advanced Dashboards, JavaScript, Computations, and Special Topics from the Experts

1. Walk through a comprehensive example of a simple, intermediate, and advanced dashboard with a focus on Interactive Reporting best practices.

2. Explore the data analysis functionally with an in-depth explanation of built-in and JavaScript functions.

3. Build custom interfaces to create batch programs and exports for automated reporting.

4. Demonstrate expertise by learning to build a central code repository.

**Getting Started with Oracle
Hyperion Planning 11**

Design, configure, and implement a robust planning,
budgeting, and forecasting solution for your organization
using Oracle Hyperion Planning

Enti Sandeep Reddy

# Getting Started with Oracle Hyperion Planning 11

ISBN: 978-1-84968-138-4          Paperback: 620 pages

Design, configure, and implement a robust planning, budgeting, and forecasting solution in your organization using Oracle Hyperion Planning

1. Successfully implement Hyperion Planning—one of the leading planning and budgeting solutions—to manage and coordinate all your business needs with this book and eBook

2. Step-by-step instructions taking you from the very basics of installing Hyperion Planning to implementing it in an enterprise environment

3. Test and optimize Hyperion Planning to perfection with essential tips and tricks

Please check **www.PacktPub.com** for information on our titles

Lightning Source UK Ltd.
Milton Keynes UK
UKOW020631041012

200018UK00003B/40/P